Praise for
Start at the End

"Did you ever wonder how some entrepreneurs have created businesses that ran by themselves, grew consistently, and sold for tons of money? Fortunately, Dave Lavinsky has created a book that outlines the steps to join this special club."

—**Robert Levin**, Editor-In-Chief,
The New York Enterprise Report

"Is your business stuck? Dave Lavinsky shows you how to *Start at the End* and achieve your dreams!"

—**Barry Moltz**, Small Business Speaker and Author

"If you want to build a sellable company, *Start at the End* will give you the road map."

—**John Warrillow**, Founder of The Sellability Score
and Author of *Built to Sell: Creating a Business
That Can Thrive Without You*

"A company needs a big vision. And then it needs a plan for reaching that vision. Read *Start at the End* and you'll quickly gain both these essential items."

—**Adam Toren**, Coauthor of *Small Business Big Vision*

"As a business owner, I wish I had read this earlier in my career. *Start at the End* makes so much sense, yet it's difficult to do tactically without this book. This book makes your business plan and dream come to life. Read it, then do it."

—**Adam Shaivitz**, Founder of Accelerate
Performance Sales Consulting and
Author of *Selling Is Everyone's Business*

START AT
THE END

START AT THE END.

HOW COMPANIES CAN GROW BIGGER AND FASTER BY REVERSING THEIR BUSINESS PLAN

DAVE LAVINSKY

WILEY

John Wiley & Sons, Inc.

Published by John Wiley & Sons, Inc., Hoboken, New Jersey.

Published simultaneously in Canada.

For general information on our other products and services or for technical support, please contact our Customer Care Department within the United States at (800) 762-2974, outside the United States at (317) 572-3993 or fax (317) 572-4002.

Wiley publishes in a variety of print and electronic formats and by print-on-demand. Some materia l included with standard print versions of this book may not be included in e-books or in print-on-demand. If this book refers to media such as a CD or DVD that is not included in the version you purchased, you may download this material at http://booksupport.wiley.com. For more information about Wiley products, visit www.wiley.com.

Library of Congress Cataloging-in-Publication Data:

Lavinsky, Dave, 1970–
    Start at the end : how companies can grow bigger and faster by reversing their business plan / Dave Lavinsky.
        p. cm.
    ISBN 978-1-118-37676-8 (cloth); ISBN 978-1-118-42173-4 (ebk);
    ISBN 978-1-118-41744-7 (ebk); ISBN 978-1-118-43446-8 (ebk)
        1. Business planning. 2. Success in business. 3. Small business–Growth.
    I. Title.
    HD30.28.L387   2013
    658.4'01—dc23

                                                                        2012022849

Printed in the United States of America

10 9 8 7 6 5 4 3 2 1

CONTENTS

INTRODUCTION

If you're like most entrepreneurs and business owners, when you first started or purchased your company, you dreamt about the finish line; specifically about how your life would be radically better once your company became a huge success.

However, soon after you launched, many of you became trapped in daily, weekly, and monthly struggles and goals: generating more sales and profits, improving employee performance, and reducing your hours and stress. At some point, virtually all of you became 100 percent focused on these short-term goals and lost sight of your long-term vision. As a result, your chances of achieving your original dreams have significantly decreased.

This book will help you turn that around.

How can I be so sure? For nearly 15 years, my company Growthink and I have helped more than 500,000 entrepreneurs and business owners start, grow, and exit their companies. Our core focus has been creating business plans that identify where companies want to go and the specific steps they need to take to get there.

We have created business plans transforming struggling companies into highly profitable ones and flat companies into high growth ones. One of our clients came to us a few years ago when the client's company was generating a few hundred thousand dollars a year in revenue but losing money. Today, this client generates more than a $100 million in annual revenue and is incredibly profitable. You can achieve such growth as well with the right plan.

I didn't always have a winning formula for creating business plans. In fact, as a serial entrepreneur I've had many failures among my many successes. I developed the right formula with the help of one of Stephen R. Covey's key principles. Specifically, in his book *The 7 Habits of Highly Effective People*, the second habit he explained was "Begin with the End in Mind." Covey stated that the key to success lies in being able to answer the question "What do you want to be when you grow up?" and then visualizing yourself achieving it. My answer to this question fluctuated over time. But it always involved a scenario in which I achieved total success, perhaps becoming a professional athlete, a highly successful businessperson, or even the president of the United States. Over time, as I learned my strengths and passions, I readjusted my answer to this question, visualized it, and progressed toward achieving it.

We have applied the *begin with the end in mind concept* with great success to help our clients achieve enhanced growth and profitability. That is, to create a winning business plan, you need to start by precisely identifying your business' end game and then start working backward to achieve it. Yes, you need to start at the end (catchy book title, huh?) and reverse engineer the success you have envisioned from that end point.

This is what you will learn in this book: How to identify what you would like your business to become and the steps you must take to get there. As you will see, you will need to shift your thinking and strategies to achieve your vision. Simply following conventional wisdom or common sense will get you common results, which means failure in most businesses, not the success you deserve.

I find it interesting that, although businesspeople often make correlations between sports and business, few businesses apply the start at the end principle engrained in sports. Let me explain.

What is the New York Giants' goal?

The answer should be easy. This team's goal each and every year is to win the Super Bowl. There's no question about this. Every player shows up for preseason training with that goal in mind. Every practice drill is performed with that goal in mind. And every game is played to win, because a win will put the team one step closer to the Super Bowl.

So, what is your company's end goal? Can you answer this question without missing a beat? Do you clearly know and understand what your organization has set out to achieve? And, equally as important: Does every employee in your organization know what this goal is?

The answer, as for so many organizations, is probably no.

But don't worry—we're going to fix that. Asking this question is a true eye-opener. In the pages of this book, we're going to uncover your answer, and when we do, your business's revenues and profits will start to take off.

Why? Because you will uncover the precise steps you need to take to achieve your end goal. You will become more focused on what really matters, inspiring your employees, and everyone involved will start making decisions that help lead the company toward its goals.

In this book, I will help you determine precisely what you'd like your business to ultimately become. You will be forced to think about your last day in business: the day you sell your company, take it public, hand it over to your children, or a similar scenario. You will also identify many of specific details of that day. How many employees will be there to say goodbye? How many customers will you be serving? What will your annual revenues be?

Once we have this detailed vision of the end, we will work backward to create a plan for you to achieve that success. Along the way, I will give you many tips and strategies you can start implementing right away to improve your sales and profits. Realizing short-term goals are crucial to long-term success because they keep us focused and energized and compel us to move towards our ultimate goal.

I want to reiterate this point: By the time you complete this book, you will have a business plan or road map for growing your business. It will include the traditional parts of a business plan, such as your marketing plan, HR plan, and financial plan and projections. Along the way, however, I will also give you marketing, leadership, and other tactics not only to put in your plan for the future but also to employ right away. I'm sure you like to see immediate results as much as I do.

In fact, when I make business decisions I always weigh both the short-term return on investment (ROI) and the long-term ROI. For example, I recently hired a firm to produce and run radio advertisements for Growthink. From a long-term ROI standpoint, I realized I wouldn't receive measurable results for at least six months, and full market saturation might take over a year. However, because the firm had great expertise in crafting compelling radio ads, I realized I could immediately get short-term ROI on the engagement by using their messages in my e-mail and online marketing. Short-term ROI and long-term ROI; that's what I demand and what I promise to give you in this text.

Here is a preview of what's to come. We will start by determining your endgame, that is, what you would like your business to achieve for you. Notice I said *achieve for you*; your business should work for you, not the opposite.

Next, we will determine the best opportunities to pursue to grow your business and attain that vision. We will then create a step-by-step action plan for you to follow by breaking down your long-term goals into shorter-term actions. Then, we will focus on improving each aspect of your business. We will systematize key functions, improve your marketing and HR plans, and give you tactics to maximize the productivity and success of your organization. Finally, we will organize everything into a business plan that will guide you and your organization to success.

This is not a book simply to be read. Instead, it offers an interactive experience to help you improve your business. To this end, you should do the following to get the most value from the book:

1. Download and complete the worksheets as you go through the book.

   The worksheets are designed to improve your understanding of the materials and help you grow your business. They are all simple to complete and force you to take action. Even if that action is as simple as writing down the end goal you'd like to achieve, the very act of documenting it will make you more likely to attain it. Your completed worksheets will become the basis of the business plan you create and follow in building the company of your dreams. All the worksheets are available at www.startatend.com.

2. In addition to learning a new approach to creating a winning business plan for your business, you will pick up many new ideas and tactics while you read.

   For example, you will learn ways to generate more customers, hire better employees, and find hidden profits in your business. Of course, you'll never realistically be able to execute all these ideas. So, circle or highlight the best ones—the ones you believe apply most specifically to your company—as you read. After you finish reading, go through the book a second time to find the ideas you highlighted. Then use these to create a list of:

a. Those you will execute within the next 7 days

b. Those you will execute within the next 60 days

c. Those you should review and possibly consider executing next year

These guidelines will not only allow you to generate a business plan that leads to the long-term success you desire; they'll also help you start increasing your revenues and profits right away. Once again, long-term and short-term ROI.

Much of the excitement you had when you first launched or purchased your business might be gone. You've now faced the sobering task of managing your company on a day-to-day basis. Fortunately, this book will rekindle your earlier excitement and your entrepreneurial spirit. It will help you regain focus and achieve the success you dreamt about when you first launched your company. You will determine exactly what you'd like your business to become and reverse engineer that success. At the end, you'll have a business plan and road map to build the highly profitable and successful company you had envisioned.

Buckle up. Your business is about to take off.

CHAPTER 1

THE END OF YOUR BUSINESS

You now know you must create a vision of your successful business. Without one, you won't know where you're headed. Once you have one, you can use it to reverse engineer a business plan for attaining it. As you'll learn in the following text, there are actually two visions you need to develop.

YOUR TWO VISIONS

Consider the words of baseball player Yogi Berra: "If you don't know where you're going, you probably won't get there."

In the case of both sports and business, he's absolutely right.

Think about that. How can you achieve your business goals if you're not crystal clear about what they are?

Therefore, the first step to improve your business's success is to write down where you want to go. We call this your *vision* or *mission*.

I'm probably not telling you anything new. You know you should have a vision statement. But 99 percent of you don't have a formal, written vision statement. You also do not have the two—yes, two—vision statements you need, nor the specificity required in each.

Let me explain.

The two types of vision statements you must develop are:

1. Your vision from a customer perspective
2. Your vision from a business perspective

Your vision from a *customer perspective* should explain what you are trying to do for your customers. It's that simple. Of course, you must know what this is before you can spell it out. For example, one restaurant's customer vision might be to "serve the best Italian food in this town." A customer vision might be more complex, as of one of my clients, Dakim, which is to "give every senior the essential tools to maintain their brain health in order to get the most out of life and help prevent the threat of memory loss."

Your vision from a *business perspective* needs to explain what your organization is trying to achieve financially.

Of course, it's great to provide the best Italian food ever. But if you go out of business while doing so, neither you, your employees, nor your customers will be happy. Therefore, you need to clearly identify your long-term vision from a business perspective. For example, do you want to sell your organization to another company eventually? Do you want to sell it to your employees? Give it to your children? Take it public? Continue to run it and reap ongoing profits?

In any of those cases, you must identify the core *financial metrics* and *business assets* your business must achieve to realize this vision. For example, how much revenue must you be generating at the time of sale to make the purchase price appealing to sell your company? How big must your customer base be?

Let's get started by documenting both your customer-focused and business-focused vision statements.

THROUGH YOUR CUSTOMERS' EYES

To reiterate, your *customer-focused* vision should explain what you are trying to do for your customers. What do you want them to gain, feel, achieve, do, and so on?

To help you understand how you might articulate this goal, the following are some famous examples of customer-focused visions (that some firms refer to as *missions*):

- Search engine Google's mission is to organize the world's information and make it universally accessible and useful.
- Nonprofit lending organization Kiva's mission is to connect people through lending to alleviate poverty.
- Renowned retailer Nordstrom's mission is to offer the customer the best possible service, selection, quality, and value.

The critical question you need to ask to create your customer-focused vision statement is: What *one thing* are you trying to do better than anyone else in serving your customers? For example, a good customer-focused vision statement could be "to provide the most environmentally friendly cleaning products" or "to provide the highest-quality automotive service" to customers.

It's also critical to add a number of customers and an end date to your customer-focused vision statement whenever possible. For instance, a financial services company might determine their mission is "to help 1 million homeowners improve their lives by getting out of debt by 2025."

You should judge your customer-focused vision statement against these questions and modify it as appropriate:

1. Will it inspire you, your employees, your customers, and potential investors or partners?

2. Does it clearly state what your company does? Keep in mind that broad claims such as "we will be the best" have little value.

3. Is it realistic and believable? Although you should think big, you should also be able to achieve your vision.

4. Is it in line with your and your company's values and culture?

For example, let's judge Nordstrom's mission of "offering the customer the best possible service, selection, quality, and value" against the following questions.

1. Will it inspire you, your employees, your customers, and potential investors or partners?

Customers are clearly inspired by Nordstrom's mission and generally pay higher prices for the superior service they receive.

Employees are also inspired and empowered by the mission, shown by the countless stories of employees going out of their way to satisfy customers. In one such case, a customer e-mailed customer service about a wedding gift purchased from Nordstrom he received years before. The gift was smoked salmon that he hadn't yet eaten. His e-mail inquired as to whether the salmon was still edible. Because Nordstrom no longer carried the product, the Nordstrom employee responded by going to a local fish market, purchasing a new jar of smoked salmon, shipping it to the customer, and telling him to throw the old product away.

2. Does it clearly state what your company does?

Although the mission doesn't specifically state that Nordstrom's business is retailing, it does clearly state that it provides its customers with the best possible service, selection, quality, and value.

3. Is it realistic and believable?

Nordstrom's mission is both realistic and believable. Although providing the best possible service, selection, quality, and value is challenging, it is attainable.

4. Is it in line with your and your company's values and culture?

Nordstrom's mission is clearly in line with its values and culture. Nordstrom values "fair and honest dealings with our customers, coworkers, suppliers, competitors, and other business partners." Its culture includes acting as a family business, empowering employees, being honest, recognizing great employees, and having fun, among other things. Nordstrom's mission and its values are clearly congruent.

Take a minute now to write down your customer-focused vision statement.

THROUGH YOUR INVESTORS' EYES

If your company has investors, their goal is most likely for your business to become wildly financially successful so they can cash out and earn a solid return on their investment.

However, your goal should be to achieve financial success even without investors. After all, a business can't achieve its customer-focused vision if it goes out of business. In such a case, it can't serve its employees or fulfill the personal desires that prompted the start or purchase of a business.

Because of this, you need to create your business-focused vision statement to show:

1. The endgame you'd like to achieve, and
2. The financial metrics and business assets you need to achieve and build to realize that endgame.

Let's look at each of these points in detail.

The Endgame You'd Like to Achieve

There will come a time when a business owner will leave the business, for many potential reasons. The business might fail, the owner might die, or the owner might sell the business. At some point, the owner will leave. Period.

It's ideal for you to leave the business under your terms. Let's define the endgame you'd prefer.

Typical endgames or exits that most entrepreneurs and business owners desire include:

• Selling the business to another entity
• Taking the business public
• Giving the business to their children
• Selling or giving the business to employees

Take a moment to think about which endgame or exit you would most like to achieve. Then think specifically about your potential date of exit and the amount for which you'd like to sell your company (or its real market value if you don't sell).

Armed with this information, now write down the endgame you'd like to achieve. Although we will fill in additional details later, for now, I just want to know (1) the date of your exit, (2) how you will exit, and (3) the dollar amount of your exit. For example, "on December 31, 2018, I will sell my business for $40 million."

The Financial Metrics and Business Assets You Need To Achieve

Now, to realize this endgame, you need to identify and achieve the requirements for success. For example, let's say that you would like to sell your business for $40 million. How much revenue must you be generating at the time of sale? How many customers must you be serving? How many employees will you have?

When you're trying to determine what your business needs to look like to earn a $40 million (or whatever amount you chose) payday, you need to consider two separate factors: *financial metrics* and *business assets*.

Financial metrics are the actual numbers that gauge your performance. Common measurements include items such as:

- Dollar revenues
- Dollar EBITDA
- Percent market share
- Number of subscribers/customers
- Number of new leads
- Percent of upsells
- Number of customer complaints
- Financial health ratios such as your current ratio

Business assets are the elements you've created that give you future economic benefits; they allow you to achieve your financial metrics. Business assets include items such as:

- Customers/marquee customers
- Products

- Services
- Technology/intellectual property
- Distribution network
- Location(s)
- Reputation/brand (trademarks/copyrights)
- Team/employees
- Financial savings via processes
- Systems/processes
- Strategic partnerships
- Plants, operating equipment
- Vehicles, furniture, real estate

The ability to understand financial metrics and business assets has a positive effect on most entrepreneurs and business owners. It forces them to stop focusing solely on financial goals (such as growing revenues and profits) and to figure out what business assets they must build to achieve those financial metrics.

Now that you understand these concepts, let's take a moment to envision the financial metrics and business assets you have achieved and built at the time of your exit.

Let me give you a fictional example. I have a small company that sells organic sunscreen. My business-focused endgame is to sell my company for $40 million on December 31, 2018.

Working backward, I know from reading industry trade journals that businesses in my sector sell on average for two times revenues. To realize my $40 million sale, I need to be generating $20 million in annual sales.

I would like to generate 25 percent earnings before interest, taxes, depreciation, and amortization (EBITDA) because that would appeal to both myself and an acquirer. So, my EBITDA goal is $5 million.

Because the wholesale price for an average bottle of organic sunscreen is $7, I will need to sell 2.85 million bottles per year to generate $20 million in sales. Because my average customer will buy 4 bottles per year, I will need to serve 712,500 customers.

To achieve these financial metrics, I will need to build significant business assets. To improve our marketing, I will need to hire a vice president (VP) of marketing who has experience taking a brand national. I will need to hire a director of public relations (PR) and social media as well as a team that reports to the director. I will also need to build a customer service team. And I will need to hire a chief financial officer (CFO) to raise money as needed and manage our finances.

To ensure uninterrupted product supply and excess capacity when needed, I must increase the size of my U.S. plant and contract with an overseas manufacturing facility. I must hire a plant manager to manage these operations.

To sell 2.85 million bottles, I will need to be in 1,200 retail locations that can sell, on average, 1,000 units per year and 6,600 retail locations that can sell, on average, 250 units per year. To accomplish this, I will need to secure six distributors and get direct accounts with select retailers such as Trader Joe's and Costco.

To sell the desired units, I will need to diversify my product line to appeal to various segments (e.g., men, women, children), so I must create these new products.

Finally, to allow the business to scale more quickly, I need to create standardized processes and systems around how employees are hired and trained, products are manufactured and quality control testing is completed, customer feedback is handled, new retailers are attracted, products are shipped to distributors, new suppliers are found and negotiated with, and new product ideas are identified and created.

To recap, the business assets and financial metrics I need to achieve are as follows:

Financial Metrics
- Revenues: $20 million   >700k
- EBITDA: $5 million
- Number of customers: 712,500   3,000 Retl

Business Assets   expm 2-%
- Products: three new products created specifically for men, women, and children
- Distribution network: 7,800 retail locations; 6 distributors; direct accounts with Trader Joe's and Costco
- Locations: two manufacturing facilities
- Reputation/brand: national awareness developed through PR and advertising
- Employees: Hire VP of marketing, PR/social media director, customer service manager, plant manager, CFO
- Systems built: marketing, production, customers, distribution, shipping, purchasing, new product development

Now envision your company at its exit. What financial metrics do you need to achieve to realize the endgame or exit vision you specified previously? What business assets do you need to build to produce these financial results?

Go to www.startatend.com to download the worksheet for creating your vision statements and document your desired financial metrics and business assets at exit.

COURAGE AND CONGRUENCY

Now you've created both your customer- and business-focused vision statement, including your (1) endgame or exit vision, (2) the financial metrics you need to achieve, and (3) the business assets you need to build.

It's important to understand that your vision statements must be aligned. You'll never reach your business goals if you don't hold true to your customer-focused vision. And you must build the right business assets to serve your customers.

In addition to ensuring your visions are aligned, your visions must become part of you, your company, and your company's culture. To achieve this, read your vision statements to yourself daily. Bring in key employees to share your visions with them. Make sure to display your vision statements for all employees to see. Post the customer-focused vision statement on your website, and share it with partners, vendors, and customers.

One company that lives their customer vision well is Zappos .com. In a daring move, many years ago Zappos eliminated its most profitable segment: drop-shipping. To avoid stocking every product, certain items were purchased on the Zappos.com website but fulfilled by manufacturers (a process known as drop-shipping). Although this was very profitable for Zappos because it incurred no inventory and storage costs, it resulted in a mediocre experience for customers because Zappos couldn't control when items were shipped.

But because Zappos' customer vision is "to provide the best customer service possible," it realized it couldn't offer this service. Although Zappos' short-term revenues and profits were hit, which put it on the brink of insolvency, long term the company flourished, aided by throngs of fully satisfied and zealous customers. Zappos' success resulted in a sale of more than a billion dollars to Amazon.com.

It takes courage to share your visions with the world. It forces you to take a stand. And often it presents a grandiose vision. Others may scoff and think you can't achieve it. The good news is that those aren't the people with whom you should associate anyway because they won't help you achieve success.

Once your vision statements become part of your company culture, magical things will happen. You and your employees will be more inspired and employee decision-making will be improved because they will be guided by your visions. There's no job manual for any position that covers every contingency. As a result, we've all heard stories of employees doing the wrong things, or going to extremes to do the right things. The latter is done when employees are guided by the right vision.

Note: Some parts of your business vision may not be appropriate to share with others. For example, you should share with employees that your goal is to achieve $X in revenue by Y date. But you may not want to share with them that you hope to sell the company at that time (they may get nervous about job security). Likewise, sharing financial metric goals with customers may not be appropriate.

A quick rule of thumb is to share any and all information you can with your constituents (employees, customers, vendors, etc.), except those items which might be misconstrued. To reiterate, telling an employee your vision is to sell your company might give that employee concerns about job security. Sharing your revenue or profit goals with customers might make them feel you are in it for the money or are offering higher prices than you should.

THE HERO'S ADVENTURE

The screenplay is complete.

You, the hero, reached your endgame and exited your company. In doing so, you dramatically grew your revenues and profits, and you built key business assets such as new products and services and a talented team of committed employees. You achieved success.

Perhaps more important, you now know precisely what this success looks like. You documented what your revenues were, what key employees you hired, how many customers you're serving, and so on.

But there's still a critical missing piece: How you're going to get there.

You see, your *vision*—which you just developed—shows *what you want*. The next step is to develop the ideal *strategy*, which shows *what you need to do*. Finally, you need to create your *plan*, which will tell you *how you will do it*.

Vision = *what* you want

Strategy = what to *do*

Plan = *how* to do it

The good news, once again, is that you just created your vision and know exactly where you're going. Creating the strategy and plan to get there will be a lot easier.

I use the term "business plan" to refer to the latter two steps: defining your strategy and putting it into an action plan. The result is a business plan that gives you the strategy and action steps you need to follow to achieve your vision.

The process of creating your business plan will also mimic reverse engineering. That is, you will start with the endgame you have envisioned and create the plan to get yourself there. Specifically, we will answer the following questions as if today was the day you achieved your endgame and you were looking backwards:

- What opportunities did you pursue that allowed you to grow most effectively?
- What marketing channels allowed you to attract or gain the most customers?

- What business partnerships (if any) have you forged that resulted in significant numbers of new clients?
- What have you done to develop your top-selling products and services?
- Who are your key managers that motivate and manage your other employees?
- What systems have you built to ensure your business runs smoothly and without your required day-to-day involvement?

We'll answer many more of these questions to ensure you have the right plans to enable your success.

PLANS RARELY COME TRUE

It's important to keep one thing in mind as we go through this: plans rarely come entirely true. Predicting the exact outcome your business will achieve is nearly impossible. But I guarantee that if you envision and plan for a $40 million company, you'll achieve more success than if you planned for a $5 million company, or worse yet, didn't plan at all.

The planning process forces you to identify the best opportunities to pursue and the best strategies to follow to get there. My favorite planning quote comes from infamous boxer Mike Tyson, who said, "Everyone's got a plan. Until they get hit." And businesses get "hit." Things don't always go smoothly and there will be ups and downs. If you have a solid plan in place, however, your business will continue to follow an upward projection and will keep proceeding toward your end goal.

In the next chapter we will start developing your ideal strategy, or what you need to do to achieve your end goal. The first step in accomplishing this will be for you to brainstorm and assess the best growth opportunities to pursue.

CHAPTER 2

CONFIRMING THE OPPORTUNITY

To recap: You've reached the point at which you know exactly where you want to go. Now we need to create the plan to get you there. Before we do this, however, we must ensure you're pursuing the right opportunities. For example, an organic sunscreen company that needs to reach $20 million in annual revenues won't get to that point by doing the same things it's doing today. Instead, it needs to identify the best growth opportunities and then execute on them.

The sunscreen company can grow by increasing penetration in natural food and product stores. It could try to penetrate the mass consumer market by seeking distribution in supermarkets and mass retailers such as Walmart or Target. It could try international expansion. It could create new products geared toward specific segments (young/old, premium/low-end, etc.). Or it could try several of these initiatives.

The number of potential opportunities the sunscreen company (and your company) could pursue is nearly limitless. You must pursue at least *one* opportunity if you want to grow and reach your end goal. Choosing the wrong opportunity could prove fatal for both small and big companies. General Motors required a government bailout after pursuing a flawed product strategy—focusing on producing bigger and faster automobiles. Conversely, other companies such as Toyota and Honda have succeeded by pursuing a different product development strategy—producing automobiles with better gas mileage.

In the following section, I will introduce you to pivoting, and why radically changing the opportunities you pursue can be advantageous. Then you will learn why strengths, weaknesses, opportunities, and threats (SWOT) analyses are essentially dead, and what to do instead to identify growth opportunities. Finally, I will show you how to judge new opportunities, because even if you execute flawlessly, going after the wrong business opportunities rarely yields success.

PIVOTING

Pivoting is the process of pursuing a different opportunity from those your company is currently pursuing. It is important to note that pivoting is often *not* the ideal strategy for your business, particularly if your business has identified a large customer need and has quality products and services to satisfy that need. However, if your business is currently struggling or not fulfilling a large customer need, you might consider pivoting. Whether or not pivoting is right for your business, I introduce the concept to show you that pursuing new opportunities has the ability to radically improve your company's success.

The following text has famous examples of companies that have pivoted or changed focus as they grew and have realized great success:

- **PayPal**, which started as a business that allowed people using handheld devices (mainly Palm Pilots) to wirelessly transfer money to each other. Based on customer feedback, it pivoted to become a business that facilitated all types of online financial transactions.

- **Adobe Systems**, which started by developing printer fonts, and later changed and grew into a complete graphics and publishing company.
- **Mattel**, which first produced picture frames. One of the company founders soon developed a side business making dollhouse furniture from the picture frame scraps. Because of the success of the dollhouse furniture, the company changed its emphasis to toys and is now the world's largest toy company.
- **Nintendo**, which originally manufactured playing cards. Over the years, Nintendo became involved in various businesses, ranging from cab companies to hotels. Nintendo first ventured into the video game industry in 1974, and started to exclusively focus on that business line a few years later.

More recently, in 2007, a small business started by Andrew Mason named The Point was formed and soon pivoted. The Point was initially formed to allow consumers to bond together to take action against companies that wronged them—to boycott them. Then Mason turned his concept around, allowing customers to bond together to get deep discounts by buying large quantities of the same product or service. The company changed its name based on its new focus, and is known today as Groupon.

Interestingly, a 2011 study released by the Startup Genome Project, which assessed more than 3,200 technology startup companies, found that the ones that pivot once or twice are much more successful. These startups had 3.6 times higher customer growth rates, and were 52 percent *less* likely to scale prematurely than startups that pivot more than two times or not at all. Once again, pivoting is particularly applicable for startups or companies that haven't yet defined or are not yet fulfilling a big customer need.

SWOTS ARE DEAD; DO A "SO" ANALYSIS INSTEAD

Business school students learn to conduct a SWOT analysis. If you're not familiar with this, it is an analysis of your business's strengths, weaknesses, opportunities, and threats.

SWOT analyses traditionally have been conducted to identify the right opportunities for you and your business to pursue. However, I'm not a huge fan of SWOT analyses in today's world. I don't think companies should dwell on their weaknesses and threats. There are constantly new threats. To meet them, you must build an incredible company that creates barriers around your customers so they stay with you long term and aren't afraid to try new things and change. Additionally, strengths-based leadership theory states that it's better to focus on your strengths than to try to improve your weaknesses.

Authors Donald O. Clifton and Paula Nelson elegantly explain this in their book *Soar with Your Strengths*, in which they wrote the following:

> The Chinese have long held the Olympic gold medal in Ping-Pong. At the 1984 Olympics, when they again captured the gold, the coach of the Chinese team was asked by a reporter, "Tell me about your team's daily training regimen."
>
> "We practice eight hours a day perfecting our strengths."

Strength based leadership

"Could you be a little more specific?"

"Here is our philosophy: If you develop your strengths to the maximum, the strength becomes so great it overwhelms the weakness. Our winning player, you see, plays only his forehand. Even though he cannot play backhand and his competition knows he cannot play backhand, his forehand is so invincible that it cannot be beaten."

Strengths-based leadership is a way to improve a company's success by focusing on and fully developing its strengths. The key to this philosophy is that people have a significantly higher ability to improve on their strengths rather than fix their weaknesses.

Makes sense, doesn't it? Most entrepreneurs and leaders do the opposite, however. They focus on improving their own and their employees' weaknesses, which only leads to frustration and bad performance. Organizations should instead look to constantly enhance their strengths so, as the Chinese ping-pong coach stated, these abilities become "so invincible that [you] cannot be beaten."

In confirming or developing new opportunities that will allow you to achieve your vision, you should conduct a SO analysis—one that focuses on your strengths and opportunities. You can undertake the process by doing the following:

1. List your organization's strengths

Brand Name -
Buying power
Loyal pts

It's helpful to first have a definition of *strength*, which can be defined as the ability to exhibit near-perfect performance consistently in a given activity.

Use this definition to create a list of the strengths that you, your company, and your employees exhibit. Examples might include:

- Company reputation or market awareness
- Assets (equipment, cash on hand, etc.)

- People
- Experience
- Location
- Product quality
- Licenses/accreditations
- Processes/systems
- Culture/morale
- Other competitive advantages

To determine the specific strengths that your company has, go through each of these sample strengths and determine whether it applies to your company.

To corroborate your assessment, survey at least one employee and one customer using the same method (i.e., going through sample strengths and seeing if they agree your company has it).

2. Rank your organization's most important strengths

Once you have your list of strengths, determine which are core to the success of your organization. For example, strengths that allow you to produce a better product or service for your customers would be critical because it can give you sustainable competitive advantage.

Search for all strengths that you can leverage when growing your company or, more important, that give your company a competitive advantage. For example, one of my colleagues is great at search engine optimization (SEO). Armed with this strength, he seeks out small manufacturing companies that could quickly grow if their websites were one of the first results shown after an Internet search. He then buys these companies and uses his SEO skills to generate many new leads and sales.

Soon thereafter, he sells them to a larger company for a significant premium.

In this case (and for your company), leveraging your strengths with the right opportunities often creates massive success.

> ### 3. Identify opportunities for growth

Brainstorm and write down all the opportunities for growth you see in your business. Generally, your opportunities will be related to:

- Developing new products or services
- Penetrating existing markets more fully (via marketing channels such as new locations, distribution channels, promotional sources, etc.)
- Targeting new customers or markets
- Establishing new marketing strategies (e.g., changing your unique selling proposition)

When thinking about new opportunities, realize that great businesses all do one thing right—they satisfy the needs of their customers. That being said, talk to your current and prospective customers and answer questions such as:

- What needs are you currently meeting?
- Can you better meet those needs with a new product or service?
- Is there a new market in which you could solve these needs?
- What related needs are you not meeting?
- Can you create a new product or service to serve those needs?

JUDGING YOUR OPPORTUNITIES

After you create your list of opportunities, you must judge each to determine the best one(s) to pursue. I recommend using several criteria to do so.

1. Judge against **your strengths**

The first criterion is to judge each opportunity against your strengths. If the opportunity leverages one of your core strengths, you'll want to pursue it because it will enhance your chances of success.

However, don't immediately discard a great opportunity that *doesn't* match your strengths. Rather, determine how easily you could acquire that strength. Could you hire an individual at a reasonable cost who would give your company the ability to develop this opportunity? Could you partner with another company that offers this particular strength? If it's something that you can acquire fairly easily, then it's an opportunity worth pursuing.

For example, at Growthink we receive a lot of phone calls. Answering the phone quickly and in a consistent manner, however, is not one of our strengths. So we found a virtual receptionist company called Ruby Receptionists. With Ruby, Growthink now has an important strength—an ability to quickly answer phone calls in a friendly and professional manner. This allows us to market our services more effectively than those with poor receptionists.

Likewise, we wanted to gain strengths in public and media relations. Simple enough; we hired a media relations manager, and the strength was ours.

2. Judge against **the Ansoff matrix**

The second criterion is to judge each opportunity using the Ansoff matrix. This tool, also called the product/market

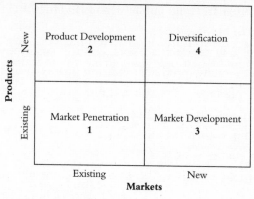

Figure 2.1   The Ansoff Matrix

expansion grid, shows the four most common ways you can grow your business.

These four methods are selling:

1. Your existing products to existing customers
2. New products to existing customers
3. Your existing products to new markets
4. New products to new markets

Graphically, you can see the Ansoff matrix in Figure 2.1.

The key to the Ansoff matrix is to understand that certain opportunities have higher risks of failure.

Selling your existing products to existing customers (market penetration—existing products, existing markets) is the least risky because you have already proven that you can do it. Opportunities here are to try new marketing channels that let you reach more customers similar to your existing customers.

For example, at Growthink, most of our customers initially found us online. From serving these customers, we knew that entrepreneurs and business owners truly wanted and liked our business plan development services. The easiest and least risky way to expand was through market penetration. Specifically, we added telemarketing, public relations, direct mail, and radio advertising to help us grow.

Offering new products to your existing customers (product development—new products, existing markets) requires that you take a bit more of a risk because you can't be sure they will buy the new products. Because you already know and have a relationship with these customers, you therefore have a relatively high chance of success.

An example of this is the smoothie company Jamba Juice expanding into frozen yogurt, teas, sandwiches, and breads to better serve its customers.

Next, offering your existing products to new markets (market development—existing products, new markets) is a bit more risky because you don't have a relationship or history with customers in those markets.

One of our clients had an industrial product it successfully sold in the food industry. It was subsequently able to launch the product in the pharmaceutical industry with great success, although doing so incurred some risk and costs.

Finally, the riskiest opportunity is to sell new products to new markets (diversification—new products, new markets). Offering a new product to a new market bears the risk of not knowing the customers or if your product or service will resonate with them. That's not to say you shouldn't try it; just that you must weigh the potential success against the increased potential for failure.

Mark each of your opportunities as a 1, 2, 3, or 4 depending on the Ansoff matrix quadrant in which they fall.

3. Judge against **the market criteria**

There are several market and marketing criteria against which you should judge your potential opportunities to determine which ones are worth pursuing. These criteria are primarily focused on new product or service opportunities you identify, and include the following:

Big market size: is the market for your potential new product or service large enough? If the market is too small, it might not make a material impact to your bottom line, even if you achieve success.

Positive market trends: is the market for your potential new product or service growing, shrinking, or flat? A shrinking market is clearly not a good indicator for your future success.

Competitive gaps: how well are competitors filling the customer needs your potential new product or service seeks to fulfill? If the answer is not very well, then how quickly or easily do you think they could modify their offerings to directly compete with you?

Solving a real pain: how big is the customer pain that your potential new product or service solves? Is your offering a "nice to have" or "*need* to have" solution?

Customer targeting: how identifiable or reachable are the customers you hope to serve with your potential new product or service? For instance, finding soccer players is easy; identifying business owners who are interested in losing weight is a bit more challenging.

4. Judge based on **financial projections**

Finally, you'll want to assess the financial implications for the top opportunities that have passed the previously listed criteria. Specifically, you should create financial projections that show the potential impact on your bottom line should you choose to pursue these opportunities.

In developing these projections, be sure to identify the resources required to execute on the opportunity (including cash and human resources), the time needed (in months) to execute on the opportunity, and best-, worse-, and average-case scenarios.

Developing accurate financial projections for each potential opportunity will help you choose the one(s) that will have the greatest return on investment for your company.

WHAT'S NEXT?

Go to www.startatend.com to download the worksheet for developing your SO analysis and determining the best opportunities to pursue.

You must determine how each opportunity ranks on the previously listed criteria and ultimately decide which opportunities have the highest likelihood of allowing you and your company to achieve your endgame.

For example, one opportunity might leverage your strengths, mesh nicely with market criteria, and have positive financial implications, but may be very risky based on its Ansoff matrix quadrant. However, this opportunity might rank above other, less risky options.

Before this chapter started, you identified where you want your business to be in the future. Upon completing the worksheet, you will know the best opportunities to pursue to get there.

In the next chapter, we will start building your strategic plan or road map to follow to achieve these objectives.

CHAPTER 3

GOALS AND MILESTONES

"A vision without a plan is just a dream. A plan without a vision is just drudgery. But a vision with a plan can change the world."

—Old Proverb

When you've decided on a long-term vision, you must identify the best ways to achieve it. One part of this is to pursue the right opportunities. The other part is to reverse engineer your vision and break it into smaller parts.

Big goals, like your endgame vision, are much more achievable when you set milestones and smaller goals. For example, if your goal is to lose 26 pounds this year, your chances of success will be much higher if you also set milestones or smaller goals of losing half a pound each week.

In your business you need to do the same. Specifically, to achieve the success you desire, you must start at the end (your desired exit vision) and work backward. Specifically, you will break down your exit vision into smaller periodic visions or goals. You will then document those goals in a business plan, which is a detailed road map for achieving your objectives.

HOW TO REVERSE ENGINEER YOUR END VISION

Reverse engineering is the process of discovering how to build something that already exists. For a product, reverse engineering typically entails taking the product apart and analyzing it to determine the best way to recreate it. For your business, reverse engineering is the process of discovering the precise steps you need to take and the goals you need to achieve to realize your business' end vision.

Let's go through the process of reverse engineering a business vision. In my organic sunscreen company example, I set my end goal as selling my company for $40 million on December 31, 2018.

I also established financial metrics; specifically, that at the time of exit, revenues would be $20 million. And I identified the business assets I needed to build, such as developing three new products and attaining six distributors.

Reverse engineering this vision is fairly straightforward; you simply work backward. If your business has achieved its vision in 5 years (e.g., $20 million in revenues, six distributors, etc.), what must it look like in four years? In three years? In two years? In one year? In six months? In one month?

As in the weight loss example, you need to set the end goal and identify smaller goals and milestones to accomplish over shorter time periods. However, unlike the weight loss example, which was completely linear (i.e., lose half a pound per week for 52 consecutive weeks), growing your business will not be linear. That is, if your revenues today are $5 million and your goal is to get to $20 million in 5 years, it is unlikely that you will grow by precisely $3 million per year. Rather, in the first year you will probably attain smaller revenue gains as you focus on building the required business assets. In later years, you will probably attain annual revenue gains exceeding $3 million.

Let me give you some examples:

- Flash sales website Ideeli (a website that offers limited-time sales on luxury items) has seen great growth over the past few years. In 2007, it generated revenues of $189,510. Then, Ideeli's sales jumped to $10 million in 2008, was nearly $50 million in 2009, and hit $78 million in 2010. Amazing growth, but not linear; in fact, sales growth has already started to slow.

- One of my clients, a services firm, grew from just over $100,000 in revenues to $5 million over three years. Rather than growing by $1.6 million per year, revenues climbed from $100,000 to $400,000 to $1.4 million to $5 million. The company had to build the requisite business assets (services, marketing/branding, etc.) during the first years, allowing it to achieve faster growth in the later years.

BREAKING YOUR END VISION INTO SMALLER PARTS

The key is to break your end vision into smaller parts, or periodic visions. In theory, if you know where you want your business to be in 5 years, or 1,825 days, you could envision where you need to be in 1,824 days, in 1,823 days, and so on, to identify precisely what you need to accomplish each day.

However, such an approach is not practical. Not only would it take too much time to complete, but your business and strategy needs evolve over time. No business operates in a vacuum, and you must be flexible and willing to change. That's why I've had the best success planning rigidly only within the near future.

Specifically, I've found that the best way to break down your business end vision is first by five years (if your exit date is beyond five years) and then one year, quarterly, and monthly.

Within each smaller time period, your goals can and will become more specific. For example, your five-year goal might be to develop three new products, and your one-year goal might be to develop one new product. Your goal in the quarter might be to conduct a survey of customers to determine what new product features and benefits they desire. And your goal in the next month might be to design the survey and identify the customers who will receive it.

Go to www.startatend.com to download the worksheets on which you will break your end vision into smaller parts. However, before you complete those exercises, let me explain more about how you will transform your end vision into more manageable and periodic goals.

 # pts rostered
 # Billings
expenses
EMR.

YOUR ONE-YEAR VISION

What goals will you accomplish this year? In documenting your vision of what you want to accomplish within the next year, be as rigorous as you were in creating your exit vision. Imagine yourself one year in the future looking back at what you accomplished. What accomplishments must you have achieved to be satisfied? What business assets have you built? What financial metrics have you realized? Your answers to these questions are your one-year vision.

Let's go back to my organic sunscreen company example. Regarding my financial metric goals, although my 5-year goal is to generate $20 million in revenues, my annual goal is to generate $1 million. Regarding profit, my goal is to pay myself $100,000 for the year and reinvest all additional profits.

Regarding my one-year business asset goals, I need to conduct market research and develop one new niche product. I must secure at least 1 new distributor and gain 1,000 new retail outlets. I must serve 35,000 customers and have 20 percent of them register on our website. I must hire a PR manager and build my brand by securing at least five major media appearances. I must contract with an overseas manufacturing facility. Finally, I must build billing and new retail store development systems to improve my operations.

Your one-year vision will progress your company closer to your five-year or exit vision even if you don't achieve it in full. It will also keep you focused on where you should spend your efforts so you are building your business rather than merely operating or administrating it.

During the next year it's possible that your one-year vision will change. Generally, a change may occur because of customer or market feedback. For example, if numerous customers say they want a product with new features, you may decide to develop that product even if new product development wasn't initially part of your one-year vision. If you see customers adopting new technologies (perhaps social media or mobile technologies) that you're not using, it may warrant adding the development of such technological capabilities to your annual plan.

However, modifying your annual vision midstream is not something to be taken lightly. I discourage it unless it is truly warranted. Modifying your vision regularly is the downfall of many entrepreneurs and business owners who constantly shift focus to pursue the newest idea and, as a result, never make real progress toward their end vision.

One of my entrepreneur friends describes these ideas as *opportunitygasms*—moments when he's essentially paralyzed by the many opportunities he sees for his business. Others refer to this as shiny object syndrome (SOS). SOS occurs when you learn or develop new opportunities, such as an interesting new idea, tactic, or strategy, that distract you from the goals or strategy you have envisioned and laid out in your business plan.

The challenge with opportunitygasms and SOS is this: Although the vast majority of new opportunities are not worth pursuing, some are. For example, if you learn of a new shift affecting your market and a new tool to help you take advantage of it, that tool might be worth pursuing even if it wasn't part of your original one-year vision and plan.

The first key is to never act immediately on your new ideas. Rather, write them down for consideration at your next planning meeting. As suggested later in this book, you will establish two planning meetings per month so you will have the opportunity to execute on new ideas quickly, although not immediately. In most cases you will find that even a week later, the once amazing idea will not be so incredible, and you'll be glad you didn't act on it.

The second key is to judge all new opportunities as *strategic* or *opportunistic*. *Strategic* means that the opportunity will likely drive your company closer to achieving its end goal as stated in your business plan.

Conversely, *opportunistic* means that the opportunity might bring in increased profits or revenues, but it doesn't drive your company toward its stated vision and goals. For example, if a company outside your industry contacts you with a partnership opportunity to launch a new product in their industry, that may prove profitable. But it might also distract you from achieving your stated goals.

In general, you should only pursue strategic opportunities. For all opportunities you come across, however, you should

Strategic vs opportunistic

write them down and consider them at your next monthly planning meeting. In that meeting you can decide whether the idea is worth adding to your business plan. More often than not, if that meeting is one or two weeks after you initially heard/came up with the new idea, the excitement of it will have worn off by then, and you'll be glad you decided not to pursue it.

YOUR QUARTERLY AND MONTHLY VISIONS

Developing your quarterly and monthly visions mimics the process of creating your one-year vision. That is, you imagine yourself one month and three months in the future looking back at what you just accomplished. And you determine what accomplishments you will be satisfied with and will have progressed you toward your end vision.

Once again, you are reverse engineering your vision. If your end goal is to create three new products and your annual goal is to create one new product, what do you need to accomplish in the next quarter and the next month to achieve this? You need to look at both the business assets you need to build and the financial metrics you must achieve.

At first, the process of creating quarterly and monthly visions is sobering for most entrepreneurs and business owners. Here's why: Although these visions are fairly easy to create, realizing them is much harder. The average business owner massively underestimates how long it takes to develop business assets. Business owners also don't realize how much time they waste administrating their business rather than growing it.

The good news is that after failing to achieve their first month's or quarter's goals, most entrepreneurs and business owners quickly adapt. They become better at setting visions and goals they can achieve, and they become more rigorous with their time so they have more to spend on critical business-building tasks.

A second challenge that most entrepreneurs and business owners face when creating monthly and quarterly visions is prioritization. Going back to the example of the organic sunscreen company, our annual vision included, among others, these four initiatives: developing a new product, gaining a new distributor, launching a PR effort, and contracting with an overseas manufacturing facility.

Clearly, not all of initiatives can be completed in one month. Even if we broke all of these initiatives into smaller tasks, we would still need to prioritize. For example, this month, would it be best for our company to complete one small task related to each of the four initiatives? Or would we be better off focusing on one initiative and progressing further on it?

The answer depends on the company and the initiatives. In many cases, the projects with the highest ROI potential should be prioritized. For example, gaining a new distributor could result in hundreds of thousands of dollars in additional sales.

However, if doing that precluded our ability to find backup manufacturing in the form of an overseas manufacturing facility, our company could be significantly hurt if something happened to our domestic facility.

Only you can weigh the potential benefits of completing and potential risks of not completing specific initiatives. Determining the right prioritization is the key task you will accomplish at your monthly planning meetings (discussed later), at which you assess your past month's and quarter's goals and actual results and create your goals and visions for the upcoming month and quarter.

In this chapter you took your end vision and broke it down into smaller, periodic visions that detailed the business assets you must build and the financial metrics you must achieve. Remember to complete the worksheets at www.startatend.com to get your detailed goals on paper.

In the next chapter, you will learn strategies to track and accomplish these financial metrics and make them an essential element throughout your company. In Chapter 5, you will learn the steps to building the business assets you envisioned.

CHAPTER 4

ACHIEVING YOUR FINANCIAL METRIC GOALS

Once you've dissected your long-term vision into smaller visions you will achieve in the next month, quarter, and year, you will gain a much clearer understanding of the actions you must take to build your business.

However, to ensure you make steady progress toward your visions, there is another essential ingredient: having a scorecard. That is, you must have a means of measuring your progress and success. If you do not, how will you ensure you are meeting your smaller visions and staying on track to achieve your long-term vision?

The good news is that you've already started to create your scorecard. I'm referring to the financial metrics you identified that you'd like to achieve. For instance, in my organic sunscreen company, these financial metrics included generating $20 million in revenues within 5 years and reaching $1 million in the next year.

In creating your scorecard, you will break out these financial metric goals even further. How? By identifying the specific actions and results you and your company need to ensure you make steady and continual progress toward your goals.

[handwritten at top: KPI' = Key Performance indicator]

MEASURING SUCCESS

The core strategy to improve your business and achieve your periodic and long-term financial metrics is to use key performance indicators (KPIs).

As the name indicates, KPIs are the metrics that judge your business's performance based on the success you would like to achieve. They serve as your scorecard.

Examples of KPIs you might want to measure in your business include:

[handwritten: ✓ T₂DM pts]

- Sales/revenues
- Number of customer leads   *[handwritten: ✓ new pt]*
- Customer conversion rates
- Number of new customers   *[handwritten: ✓ new onctt pt]*
- Number of subscribers
- Number of PR mentions   *[handwritten: ✓ CHF pts]*
- Number of website visitors   *[handwritten: ✓ Bipolar,]*
- Number of products manufactured   *[handwritten: schis· pts]*
- Amount and percentage of cost of goods sold
- Amount and percentage of marketing costs   *[handwritten: ✓ ↑]*
- Amount of inventory levels
- Amount of accounts receivable   *[handwritten: MLM]*
- Amount and percentage of net income   *[handwritten: BB]*
- Amount of cash   *[handwritten: PAP,]*
- Percentage of employee turnover
- Number of new employee hires
- Amount of payroll   *[handwritten: JO]*
- Number and percentage of product defects
- Percentage of customer satisfaction
- Number of key financial/operating ratios, such as current ratio, quick ratio, debt ratio, asset turnover ratio, sales/working capital ratio, and so on.

[handwritten: prevalable (on]

Let me give you a personal example of why tracking these KPIs is so important. In one of my businesses, we started expanding our marketing expenditures. As a result, the number of leads we started getting grew dramatically. We were getting more telephone calls and more prospects were e-mailing us and filling out forms on our website.

When the month ended and we tallied our sales, however, our results were flat. Although we had nearly 40 percent more leads than the previous month, our sales remained the same. What turned out to be the culprit? Our customer conversion rates. In the previous month, approximately 40 percent of our prospective clients said "yes" to our proposals. In the current month, however, that number dropped to 30 percent (probably because our sales team wasn't used to handling so many leads).

Had we not tracked our KPIs and discovered that the problem was our customer conversion rates, we wouldn't have been able to fix it. Because we did track it, however, we were able to fix it. We determined ways to more quickly and expertly create and deliver our proposals. Our proposal conversion rate climbed back up to 40 percent, and with the increased number of leads, our sales and profits flourished.

WHY YOU NEED KPIS

KPIs serve several core purposes.

First, they allow you to set goals and judge your performance against them.

For example, let's say that your sales goal for next month is $100,000. Tracking sales as a KPI would let you know whether you met that goal. It would also let you know you were on track to meet the goal. For example, if your sales were less than $50,000 on the 15th of the month, you'd realize you were behind schedule.

Second, and perhaps more important, KPIs allow you to manage and improve performance on underlying issues. For example, in your business, sales volume might be a function of (1) the number of cold calls your sales team makes, (2) the number of proposals given to prospective clients, (3) the percentage of prospective clients who say "yes" to proposals (your proposal conversion rate), and (4) the average sales price.

In this case, each of these four KPIs are underlying issues that impact your sales and so must be tracked. For example, you would probably notice a decrease in revenues if your proposal conversion rates decreased (as in my example). If so, you could take corrective action to fix the problem. Conversely, if you weren't tracking proposal conversion rates, you wouldn't know what caused the sales decline and you'd be helpless.

KPIs, when monitored periodically (i.e., weekly or monthly), allow you to know what's going on in your business and alert you to problems before it's too late.

KPIs make managing your business easier because they numerically measure performance throughout your business. This allows you to more easily manage the business and take more time off because micromanagement is unnecessary. For instance, if the number of customer complaints is low, you know your fulfillment team is performing well.

Finally, KPIs serve as a great management tool. If employees know they are being judged on a specific KPI (e.g., your PR person is judged on the number of media mentions they achieve), they will be more focused on successfully achieving those goals.

Tracking KPIs is critical to achieve the financial metrics you established in your vision. You and your team will know if you're reaching the metrics, and you'll learn which underlying issues you must focus on to boost results.

BUILDING YOUR SCOREBOARD

Earlier, I talked about the New York Giants and how their singular goal every year is to win the Super Bowl. In trying to achieve this vision, the Giants rely heavily on scoreboards.

One type of scoreboard they use is the League standings that show their record and how many more wins they need to make the playoffs.

Another scoreboard the Giants use is the traditional game scoreboard in the stadium that tells the current score of each game and the time left. Clearly, this scoreboard is necessary for the Giants to make strategic decisions on what to do next to win that game.

The Giants also use a list of detailed player statistics. This scoreboard shows which running backs are getting the most carries and for how many yards, which receivers are being most productive, and which quarterbacks are doing well. These data are also critical in judging the team's performance and determining what changes are needed for improvement.

Just like the scoreboards that the Giants use, your business needs a scorecard. In business, we refer to this scorecard as your "financial dashboard." Your financial dashboard is simply a listing of all your KPIs and their results. Once you determine which KPIs to track, you can then quickly and easily review your dashboard periodically to judge the financial health and performance of your business, and to make changes when needed.

1. Which KPIs to Include in Your Dashboard

Go through the previously listed sample KPIs. Which KPIs are applicable for your business? What other KPIs would help you manage your business? What metrics would you like to improve (e.g., sales, number of product returns, customer satisfaction, etc.)? Each of these metrics should be in your list of KPIs.

To find even more KPIs for your business, answer these questions:

Imagine there are five direct competitors in your business, and that you were given a blank check and the ability to buy any of these companies. As a result, each of these companies opened up their books to you and answered any questions you asked them. What key metrics would you look at in each company to determine which to buy? Which would offer the greatest value?

Each of these metrics should be KPIs in your dashboard.

Let me give you an example. You and I decided to go into business together by purchasing a pizza shop. We found three pizza shops that were being sold. In determining which business to buy, we would probably ask questions such as the following:

- What were your revenues last year? What are your revenues so far this year? (Are revenues going up or down?)
- How many phone calls do you get each day?
- What is your average order size? (If the average order size is low, it might be an easy opportunity to grow revenues and profits by increasing it.)
- How many repeat customers do you have? What revenues do they generate? (The more repeat customer revenues the better because they will probably keep buying from us and ensure solid revenues.)
- What is your monthly advertising budget and where is it being spent? (If no budget or a small advertising budget, there may be a big opportunity to grow with strategic advertising.)

As you can see, armed with these KPIs, we could determine how valuable the business is and how to increase its value.

2. How Often to Measure Each of Your KPIs

You need to view all of your KPIs on a regular basis.

Some KPIs need to be viewed daily; others may be viewed weekly or monthly. For example, a KPI for your company may be how many outbound calls your sales team makes. You may want to measure this daily or weekly. You probably don't want to measure it monthly because if the numbers are too low, you want to correct the problem quickly. Conversely, you may only need to measure your advertising expenses monthly.

Identify the frequency with which you will measure each of your KPIs.

3. Against What You Should Measure Each of Your KPIs

The final question you need to answer is against what you should measure each of your KPIs. For example, if today were May 12th and your monthly sales so far totaled $84,617, how could you tell whether this is good or bad? That's why you need other figures with which to compare your KPIs.

For example, you could compare your May 1st through May 12th sales results to:

- Previous month's results (e.g., April 1st through April 12th)
- Current month's projections (e.g., my forecast for May 1st through May 12th)
  - Essentially this would be your May sales goal divided by 31 (to get a daily average) and multiplied by 12 (to get what May 1st through May 12th sales should be if you were on track)
- Last year's results (e.g., May 1st through May 12th of the previous year)

You might have multiple metrics against which you measure each of your KPIs. These metrics might include past results, future goals, or industry standards or benchmarks.

4. Document Your KPIs

Using the following chart, you can identify the KPIs you will track, how often you will track them, and against what you will judge your performance.

Key Performance Indicators (KPIs)	Frequency	Versus

5. Maintaining Your Financial Dashboard

Finally, you need to choose the program in which you will maintain your financial dashboard.

The simplest program is a spreadsheet program such as Microsoft Excel. In this spreadsheet, you list the KPIs in the first column and then the results in subsequent columns. In doing so, you might categorize the KPIs based on their function (e.g., sales KPIs, fulfillment KPIs, etc.) and the frequency you update them, and ensure the relevant figures that you're comparing each KPI against are shown.

Another option for your financial dashboard program is to use a program such as Google Documents. Google Documents offers a spreadsheet program hosted online that multiple users can view and update simultaneously. This makes it easier to update and view the KPIs (and to avoid multiple documents being passed around).

You may want to invest in financial dashboard software; either software that's "off the shelf" or customized for your business. Such software can often use application programming interfaces (APIs) that automatically pull figures from certain places (e.g., it automatically pulls your payroll figures from your payroll software, your revenue figures from you accounting software, etc.). Doing so simplifies and automates the process of maintaining your financial dashboard.

Finally, you need to choose the person who will be responsible for creating or updating your financial dashboard. It cannot be you. Although the financial dashboard will be invaluable to your company, the work involved in maintaining it is "data gathering"—important work, but not the $500+/hour work you must be doing as a business owner (i.e., coming up with new marketing ideas, systematizing your business, training people, etc.).

Typically, you will want one person in your company to be responsible for maintaining the dashboard. You will need to let others know that they must assist that person. For example, your sales manager (who probably won't be the person maintaining the dashboard) will have to provide sales-related data.

Go to www.startatend.com to download worksheets to help you build your financial dashboard.

The key to running a great business is to effectively manage the business. Without KPIs and a scorecard, effective management becomes nearly impossible. For example, could the coach of the New York Giants manage his team without looking at the stats? Clearly not.

Once you and your team know the KPIs on which to focus, your business can grow. Everyone will know what to do, what to focus on, and what constitutes success (i.e., improving performance on the KPIs). This eliminates the need for you to micromanage and allows you to focus on further growing your business.

Now that you understand how to achieve your *financial metric goals*, you need to learn how to best achieve your *business asset goals*. We will cover this in the next chapter.

CHAPTER 5

ACHIEVING YOUR BUSINESS ASSET GOALS

As you may recall, business assets are the valuable resources your business must create to achieve the financial metrics you desire. For example, without building a customer base (a key business asset), you will not be able to grow your sales. Other common business assets required to grow include new products and services, distribution networks, intellectual property, customers, locations, strategic partnerships, and your team, among others.

Your first challenge is to determine which assets to build and when. For example, a few years ago I looked at my business and identified a series of business assets I needed. I needed to create and launch several new products and services, hire and train three key managers, and build national credibility through PR. I also needed to implement systems to more easily run the business so I could take more vacations and spend more time with my family. Without these business assets, I would not be able to grow my business.

Although I had identified the right business assets that would allow me to grow, creating them was, at first, a daunting task because they led to several questions such as: How do I create these assets? Which one(s) should I create first? If I create these assets, will my short-term results suffer?

This chapter answers these questions and more so you can build the required business assets that allow you to achieve both your short-term and long-term visions.

BUSINESS ASSETS VIA PROJECT MANAGEMENT

The key to building business assets is to use structured project management techniques. Project management is the process of achieving goals via planning, organizing, securing, and managing resources. A project is defined as a temporary undertaking with a specific beginning and end.

Each of the business assets you create should be treated as projects. For example, although you might want to secure an unlimited number of distributors to sell your product, it is more effective to set up a project to find and secure 50 distributors. Once you have achieved that, you could establish a new project to find and secure 100 more, and so on.

For example, one of my clients wanted to raise venture capital to fund their business. To fulfill this goal, we identified the business assets they required. These included (1) investor presentation materials (investor business plan, executive summary, and slide presentation), (2) beta customers, and (3) a fuller management team. With these business assets, my client would be in the best position to raise venture capital.

We further broke the development of these assets into smaller projects. Projects included:

- Putting together the investor materials
- Creating a comprehensive list of venture capitalists
- Contacting and presenting to the venture capitalists
- Creating a list of prospective beta customers

- Contacting and presenting to prospective beta customers
- Creating job descriptions of ideal management team additions
- Networking to find referrals to potential management team additions
- Interviewing and hiring new managers

Some of these projects were completed simultaneously, whereas some were done one after the other. The result? By identifying, planning, and completing these projects, we built the requisite business assets and were able to successfully raise the venture capital and build a great company.

ENTREPRENEURIAL PROJECT MANAGEMENT

Scores of textbooks have been written on effective project management. Unfortunately, most of them are meant for large organizations with big budgets. Those strategies don't always work in a smaller setting. In a smaller setting, project management works by breaking the larger project into attainable pieces, with each piece contributing to the whole.

Our goal here is to cut to the chase—to give you project management techniques you can learn and implement quickly to build the business assets your company needs. As a small business owner or startup, you have limited time and resources and need results.

Project management is a task that's best mastered when broken into parts. Here are the five steps you should follow to execute on projects and most effectively build the business assets your company needs:

Step 1: Define the nature and scope of the project

Step 2: Assign a project manager

Step 3: Plan out the project

Step 4: Execute and monitor the project

Step 5: Conduct post project reviews

Step 1: Define the Nature and Scope of the Project

This step is fairly straightforward: You identify the project (e.g., finding 10 more distributors for your product). In this step you should set key criteria such as:

- What are the characteristics of distributors you want?
- How long should the project take?
- What budget (if any) there is to complete the project?
- Who in your company (if not you) will manage the project?

Step 2: Assign a Project Manager

In this step you will assign the person who will manage or direct the project. Clearly, the choice of project manager will impact the project's success, so choose the person with the most appropriate skill set.

Note that the person may be a full-time employee, an outside firm, or a contractor. In choosing which to use, consider the nature of the project. For example, if the project is to build a product that requires unique skills and insight into your business, likely it can be best built by a full-time employee who knows your business and customers.

Conversely, if you are looking to build a billing solution to systematize the billing of your clients, it's probably most efficient to hire an outside firm or contractor who specializes in that area.

Once you determine the appropriate project manager, go through the nature and scope of the project with them and get their full buy-in.

Step 3: Plan out the Project

The next step is to sit down with the project manager to plan out the project. The first thing you should do is identify the most likely obstacles that will be faced during the project.

This is a crucial step that is generally overlooked. Be sure to spend a few moments determining potential problems so you can create contingency plans beforehand.

After identifying potential obstacles, break down the project into smaller pieces or specific tasks that must be accomplished. In this example, these tasks might include:

- Creating a list of potential distributors
- Rating each potential distributor on qualifications criteria
- Choosing the potential distributors to target
- Selecting/hiring sales staff to call on distributors
- Sending letters to potential distributors
- Attending face-to-face meetings with potential distributors
- Going to five trade shows to meet potential distributors
- Advertising in three trade journals for four months each

This month your goal might be to create the list of potential distributors. By the end of this quarter, your goal might be to also hire one new salesperson, advertise in one trade journal, attend one trade show, and make five face-to-face sales calls to potential distributors.

In planning out your projects, particularly those that will take more than one month to achieve, you need to break down your plans by month and quarter to ensure you stay on track.

Step 4: Execute and Monitor the Project

Particularly if you are not the project manager, you must stay abreast of each key project in your company. Have your project manager identify specific deliverables or milestones when individual tasks must be accomplished. Set up meetings with your project manager after these milestones are due to ensure they were accomplished, and offer suggestions for improvement.

Step 5: Conduct Post Project Reviews

Most entrepreneurs and business owners fail to do this last step. Unfortunately, it's often the most important.

At the end of each project, you should meet with the project manager to discuss what went right, what went wrong, and what changes should be made during the next project he or she manages.

Providing open feedback better trains your team to manage projects so future projects are completed more efficiently and effectively.

CHOOSING AND MANAGING YOUR PROJECTS

Which business assets should you build and which projects should you start? Once again, you can choose which projects to launch by working in reverse. That is, go back to the one-year, quarterly, and monthly business asset goals you documented previously—the goals that when achieved will bring you to your exit vision.

Start by assessing the list of business assets you need to develop in the upcoming year. Next, prioritize them to identify the ones that need to start immediately and the ones that can wait. Then, you need to establish projects for each business asset (e.g., define the nature and scope, plan out, etc.).

As you might imagine, this quickly gets fairly complex because you will have several project managers and multiple tasks. Certain projects also might be dependent on other projects. For example, if your goal is to take a new product to market, you need to both develop the product (project 1) and begin marketing it (project 2). Clearly, parts of project 2 can't be completed until project 1 is complete.

Because of this complexity, I recommend you use a Gantt chart to organize your projects. A Gantt chart illustrates how projects will be completed. It shows interrelations between and within projects. In your Gantt chart, you should identify all the projects that need to be developed and the specific tasks within each project that need to be completed.

In the chart, you will assign a project manager (the person in your company who is responsible for completing it) to each project, and assign a completion date. Your Gantt chart will enable you to manage the completion of all the projects and tasks that allow you to build your business assets and achieve your vision.

Let's take a closer look at the Gantt chart you need to develop. Figure 5.1 is the Gantt chart for the venture capital example I used earlier.

As you can see, we identified three core projects we needed to complete: develop investor materials and contact, gain beta customers, and build management team. The Gantt chart details a project manager for each project, and identifies specific activities and tasks and the person responsible for each.

Following the chart, we were able to start and complete tasks within each of the three core projects in January. Once these tasks were completed, we moved onto new tasks. As of the end

Project: Develop Investor Materials & Contact										
Project Manager: Dave										
Task/Activity	Person Responsible	Status	Jan	Feb	Mar	Apr	May	Jun	Jul	Aug
Write business plan & executive summary	Dave	In-progress								
Create investor slide presentation	Sally	Starting								
Create list of venture capitalists	Greg	Starting								
Contact and present to venture capitalists	Greg	Waiting to Start								
Finalize agreement/receive financing	Greg	Waiting to Start								
Project: Gain Beta Customers										
Project Manager: Roger										
Task/Activity	Person Responsible	Status	Jan	Feb	Mar	Apr	May	Jun	Jul	Aug
Create list of prospective beta customers	Tom	Complete								
Contact/present to beta customers	Roger	Starting								
Secure beta customers/complete paperwork	Roger	Waiting to Start								
Project: Build Management Team										
Project Manager: Jen										
Task/Activity	Person Responsible	Status	Jan	Feb	Mar	Apr	May	Jun	Jul	Aug
Create job descriptions	Dave	Complete								
Network and ask for referals	Roger	In-progress								
Conduct interviews	Jen	Starting								
Hire/complete paperwork	Jen	Waiting to Start								

Figure 5.1   Gantt Chart

of January, the status of each task was updated to show which tasks were completed, which were in-progress, which were starting, and which had not yet commenced.

As you can see in Figure 5.1, we didn't plan or try to contact venture capitalists until April, after all of the projects were completed. Importantly, by planning and mapping out the individual projects and tasks within the Gantt chart, we completed everything in a timely fashion and succeeded in raising venture capital.

WHY GREAT PROJECT MANAGEMENT WILL CHANGE YOUR LIFE (OR AT LEAST YOUR BUSINESS)

The key to any company's success are the business assets it has built. For a company such as Apple, its cool and cutting-edge products are its key asset. For Zappos.com, its culture and team is a key asset. For Verizon Wireless, its massive customer base and contracts with these customers is a key asset.

In each case, these business assets give these companies the ability to generate significant revenues and profits in the future. The same is true for your company. And the key is choosing the right assets to build and building them most effectively.

In choosing which assets to build look to your short-term and long-term visions that identified how your company will look in one to five years. That exercise helped you determine which business assets you developed and when. The challenge arises when you have multiple business assets to complete during a certain period (e.g., within the next month, quarter, or year). In this case, you need to prioritize. I prefer to prioritize those assets that yield more short-term benefits and ROI so you can reap the rewards sooner. However, in certain cases, the natural ordering of assets will choose their priority; for example, if you first need to develop a product before you can build your distribution network.

To build your business assets most effectively, use the project management techniques explained in this chapter. They will boost your business's success because they will allow you to rapidly grow. They will change your life because building these assets forces you to act and think strategically and long term, rather than spending too much time every day fighting the fires that arise in most businesses.

If you asked most business owners what they accomplished in their business last month, most would give you a blank stare. Most of them accomplished very little. Maybe they increased sales or profits a bit, but they spent most of their time managing their day-to-day operations. You, on the other hand, will be able to point to the key business assets you developed the month prior. These assets will enable your business to thrive. For example, business assets such as new systems, products, and trained employees will allow your business to run more smoothly. They will boost your sales and profits and give you a sustainable competitive advantage, which will massively increase the value of your company to potential acquirers down the road.

Go to www.startatend.com to download a spreadsheet you can use to build your Gantt chart.

CHAPTER 6

SYSTEMATIZING YOUR BUSINESS

How fast does your business move? How many mistakes do your employees make? Armed with the right business assets, such as great products, a highly trained team, and a large customer base, achieving success should be fairly easy, unless your team moves slowly and makes mistakes.

For example, if Apple often shipped customers the wrong product, the company would falter. If it took twice as long to develop and introduce new products, sales and profits would dip considerably.

As you know, Apple doesn't exhibit these flaws. Why? Because Apple, like most great companies, has developed multiple systems that dictate how it completes vital functions such as hiring and training employees, processing orders, and managing customer experiences. Systems are an extremely valuable business asset that allow you and your company to reach its goals.

Systems allow you to progress faster and with more consistency. Conversely, without systems things can and will go wrong. As an example, consider the ordering systems most restaurants use today. Waiters and waitresses can now take your order on a handheld device. They can also take your order on paper and easily enter it on a touch screen computer.

The results? Among other things, these systems automatically calculate customer bills. Conversely, I remember as a teenager recalculating handwritten bills in my head and finding mistakes. These systems also prevent ordering mistakes, such as cooks being unable to read the handwriting on written orders or waiters delivering meals to the wrong tables. Because the systems automatically show orders to the cooking staff, orders also get fulfilled faster. They allow owners to better manage their restaurants; the owners can quickly see what the top-selling items are, which items they need to restock, whether there are any inconsistencies that may indicate employee theft, and so on.

Clearly, the restaurant's management systems allow it to perform faster and with more consistency. This better satisfies their customers and reduces costs, which is exactly what restaurant owners want.

The term *system* applies to much more than technology systems like restaurant ordering software. In fact, systems can and should apply to virtually every aspect of your business. When applied properly, your business can and will flourish.

INTRODUCTION TO SYSTEMS

A system is a procedure or process for obtaining an objective or completing a task. That's the basic definition. When you truly systematize your business, you'll describe a system as the way you get things done.

In some cases, these processes are very sophisticated and may require an engineer or technician to develop them, such as the restaurant ordering system mentioned earlier. In most cases, however, the processes are simply documented and methodical ways of completing an objective, such as how to handle phone calls or how to make your company's products.

When you think about it, your entire business is one big system. If so, wouldn't it be great to fully systematize it so it runs like clockwork?

There are several reasons why you'd want to build systems and processes in your business. The main ones are:

1. *Precision and consistency.* By having set processes for how tasks should be completed, you will get consistent quality results.

2. *Time and money savings.* When employees know precisely how to do something and do it the same way each time, they eventually become much better and faster at performing the task. This saves time and money, and gives you a competitive advantage.

3. *Scalability.* When you have set processes for completing tasks, it's much easier to hire and train new employees and grow your business.

4. *Free your time and build business value.* Developing and implementing systems allows your business to run without you. This frees up your time to focus on building your business further (and taking time off) and makes your business more attractive and valuable to potential acquirers (because it's not dependent on you and the acquirer can see how the business could continue to scale and provide value).

A business's ability to run without its leader deserves further clarification and is why systems are perhaps the most important business asset you must build. The single biggest problem in virtually any small business is *you*—the head entrepreneur, business owner, or department head. This is because you are the restraint or bottleneck.

Because there's not enough of you to go around, things don't get done. You're probably the best at coming up with new product ideas, spotting new marketing opportunities, and so on. Because you can only work so many hours in a day, many of these critical tasks just don't get done.

The beauty of developing systems is that they allow you to put structures in place to get things done using less of your time. Imagine if you had a system for new product development and all you had to do was come up with the idea and the system would create it. In this situation, you'd have time to develop many new and great product ideas.

Most entrepreneurs and business owners have a negative view on systems because they think they are difficult to establish. I'd like for you to view systems in a different way. Using systems, *you* become the customer.

Think about that. If your company has a system for creating new products with minimal involvement from you, who then is the customer? Who benefits the most? You do. If your company has a system for following up with customers to ensure 100 percent customer satisfaction, which results in referrals and repeat business, who benefits? Once again, you do.

Although systems do take time and energy to build, they directly benefit you. If you ever want to sell your business, they benefit the new owner, who will happily pay a handsome premium for them.

One example of a system that allowed a company to scale well is Google's hiring system. In January of 2000, Google had fewer than 100 employees. The number of employees grew to more than 250 a year later, then to 500 at the start of 2003. By the end of 2004, Google had more than 3,000 employees, and by the end of 2005 it had nearly 6,000 employees.

When hiring thousands of employees per year, you need systems in place, unless you want to make lots of mistakes and wind up

with the wrong employees and culture. That's why Google established a comprehensive hiring system that included multiple steps.
After job applicants complete an online form, a Google screener
reviews their application to determine initial fit. Applicants who
make it through that process then complete a phone interview.
This is followed by on-site interviews in which applicants are typically interviewed by four or five Google employees for 45 minutes
each. Google also has additional tests and evaluations for engineering and nonengineering roles, such as completing sample work.

After this, the Google interviewers submit their thoughts to a
hiring committee, who must come to a consensus. After a consensus is reached, the candidates are reviewed by senior-level
management, discussed at a compensation committee review
meeting, reassessed by senior-level management, and then finally
given an offer.

Clearly, this is a very comprehensive system that is costly to
execute and not required by most entrepreneurs and small business owners. But it is a system that worked for Google and
allowed it to grow to one of the largest companies in the world.
Imagine you had such foolproof systems for all aspects of your
business. You'd be unstoppable.

However, although most systems do not require nearly the
complexity, time, and cost of Google's hiring systems, most entrepreneurs and business owners don't create systems. Generally
they have two poorly reasoned excuses:

1. Systems take too long to build.
   It does take considerably longer to build a system than
   to simply perform once the task the system is designed to
   accomplish. However, if the task is often repeated or you
   will need the task to be completed by someone new, having a system in place will pay for itself.
2. There are too many exceptions to the rule.

For example, you might think that you can't build a system for handling inbound calls because there are too many possible things about which your customers could inquire. This is precisely why you need systems, however. As you grow your company, you will become farther removed from daily tasks such as answering phones or responding to e-mails. The process of systematizing your business forces you to address multiple scenarios, and eliminate some or all exceptions to the rule.

WHAT SYSTEMS TO CREATE IN YOUR BUSINESS

Systems are established ways of doing things that allow you to reap advantages such as increased consistency, savings in time and money, and more time for you to grow your business.

So what should you systematize in your business? You should systematize any process in your business that is performed frequently, and that, if completed in a predictable, consistent manner, would increase the value and profits of your business. Likewise, any process that can free up your time should be systematized.

Examples of areas within your business that you could systematize include:

- Product development (i.e., how you manufacture products)
- Service delivery (i.e., how you deliver your services)
- Purchasing (i.e., how you find products to buy and negotiate with vendors)
- Marketing (i.e., how you design advertisements and find media in which to place them)
- Sales (i.e., how you buy lists of prospects)

- Hiring (i.e., how you find, screen, and hire new employees)
- Training (i.e., how you train new employees)
- KPI reporting (i.e., how you maintain your financial dashboard)
- Bookkeeping (i.e., how you record debits and credits)
- Legal (i.e., how you respond to legal issues)
- Customer service (i.e., how you solve customer service issues)
- Inbound phone calls (i.e., how you answer and route incoming phone calls)
- New product development (i.e., how you generate new ideas and commercialize them)
- Customer management (i.e., how you maintain relationships with current customers and keep them satisfied)
- Technology management (i.e., how you keep up with the latest technology trends and products and implement them in your business)
- Customer referrals (i.e., how you ensure all customers are asked to provide referrals)
- Pricing (i.e., how you determine pricing for products and services and when to change them)

You don't always need to create the systems yourself. In the restaurant ordering software example used earlier in the chapter, you could simply purchase the solution from a vendor. Using the previous examples, and thinking through the processes your business performs frequently, write down (right now) a list of key processes you must systematize in your business. Then mark the ones you might be able to attain from an outside vendor (e.g., bookkeeping or inventory management software) and the ones you will need to develop internally.

THE PROCESS OF CREATING SYSTEMS

Creating systems is mostly a documentation exercise. That is, you simply document how you would like the process to be performed. When doing so, you need to account for all possible scenarios.

For example, creating your system for handling inbound phone calls might include:

- Identifying whether the caller is a current or prospective customer
- Asking the caller for certain information (e.g., name, telephone number, etc.)
- Identifying the different prompts for the caller to press (e.g., press 1 for customer service, press 2 for sales, etc.)
- Determining if you want to have a live operator or an automated system to route calls
- Identifying who should answer the calls once they are routed (e.g., who answers sales requests, customer service requests, etc.)
- Determining how long a caller should have to wait until their call goes to voice mail
- Determining your call-back policies (within what time period all calls must be returned)
- Documenting phone scripts for multiple inquiries
- Determining how calls should be documented (e.g., add callers to your customer relationship management [CRM] database, document each call in a text document, etc.)
- Determining the goals for each call (e.g., to get the sale, to get their name/number, to get them to come into the store, etc.)

In this handling inbound phone calls system example, you probably want your system to also include an if/then flowchart showing the different scenarios that might arise. For example, the flowchart would show that *if* the customer presses "2" for sales, *then* he would go to a sales department associate, who answers with this script, and so on.

Process Maps

Flowcharts that are used to map out processes, such as the one mentioned previously, are known as *process maps*, and they are the cornerstone to systems development.

To develop a process map, you must start with the beginning of the process to be completed. Then picture the ideal outcome. Finally, determine every step in between to reach that ideal outcome. In developing process maps, specific symbols are used, mainly ovals, rectangles, diamonds, and lines, as seen in Figure 6.1.

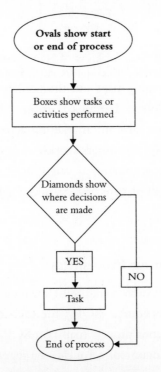

Figure 6.1   Process Map

Figure 6.2   Process Map for Flow of New Customers

A big picture system maps out the general process that your company should follow. Figure 6.2 is an example big picture process map for your sales and marketing department that shows how the flow of new customers works.

A small picture system maps out specific processes. Figure 6.3 is a sample small picture process map for handling inbound phone calls.

Standard Operating Procedures

The next step in systematizing your business is to create standard operating procedures (SOPs) for each of the key activities performed in your process maps. An SOP is a set of written instructions that document a routine or repetitive activity that your employees must follow.

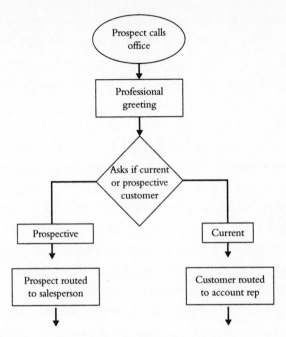

Figure 6.3   Process Map for Inbound Phone Calls

By having SOPs, you ensure consistent high performance in your company. For example, within the process of handling inbound phone calls, you should have an SOP document stating how the phone should be answered (e.g., "Hi, this is [name]. Thank you for calling XYZ Company. How can I help you?")

Likewise, that SOP document should detail the appropriate answers to frequently asked questions.

Policies and Guidelines

You don't need and can't have SOPs for every situation or scenario an employee comes across. Rather, SOPs and systems are focused on improving results on frequently performed processes.

For outliers and processes that are not frequently performed, your company should have stated policies and guidelines. For example, if a client e-mails a question, what is the required turnaround time on a response? What salutation should your employees use when responding?

These are mechanisms that customers and clients don't always realize are in place, but smooth communication changes their perception. Think about companies such as Nordstrom and the example I gave you earlier of the Nordstrom employee who purchased a new jar of smoked salmon for a customer who had questions about an old jar. I used that example to illustrate the power of Nordstrom's culture and customer-focused vision statement. But to create this culture, Nordstrom had to create the right policies and guidelines.

In this case, the employee's actions fell squarely within the guidelines. But what if the employee had decided to purchase and send the customer a $1,000 jar of salmon? Would that have been appropriate? Would Nordstrom have compensated the employee? Certainly not, because compensating the customer with something of significantly higher value than the original purchase would be outside its policies and guidelines.

Most companies don't set policies and guidelines. As a result, employees are clueless as to the right way to do things and often perform poorly as a result. Create policies and guidelines that set expectations and help employees make the best decisions.

GETTING STARTED WITH SYSTEMATIZING YOUR BUSINESS

Right now you are probably thinking that creating systems and the process maps, SOPs, and policies and guidelines that comprise them is a daunting task.

I won't sugarcoat it; it will take time and energy. However, the benefits far outweigh the costs.

For example, I'm sure you can imagine how smoothly your company would run if the 5, 25, 100, 500, 1,000, or even 10,000 employees you have had a way to learn how every key task should be performed.

They would perform tasks expertly and consistently. They would wow your customers. They would outperform your competitors. They would save time and money and thus boost your profits. They would allow your business to run without your day-to-day involvement. And they would attract tons of potential acquirers who would want to buy the massive value you created.

The first step in systematizing your business is to build one system. Start small, but think big. If you're going to start by creating just one system, it should be one that can really impact your results.

In general, the system that can best boost your results is a system for your company's biggest functional bottleneck. For many companies, it's their ability to attract new customers. For others, it's getting more business from existing clients. For still others, it's performing the service it sells.

Identify the one bottleneck stifling your growth right now. Then create a system around this process. For example, if your bottleneck is converting prospective customers into paying customers, map out the system to improve it. Create the process maps, SOPs, and guidelines. Then distribute them to your employees and train them on the new procedures.

After one system is in place, you should identify other key systems to build in your business. As you might have imagined, as you grow your business, new systems will always need to be built.

MAKING A SYSTEM THE STATUS QUO

Each time you or one of your employees creates a new system, be sure to add the documentation to a systems binder. Buy a three-ring binder, and every time a new system is developed, print it out and add it to the binder.

Periodically, you should review each system by reading through the binder. Doing so will alert you to new ideas to improve your systems to become more efficient and profitable. It will also alert you to other systems that need to be built.

In addition to the physical binder of systems, you should maintain a digital copy of them so that you can more easily distribute the information, update the systems, and print new copies.

I explained earlier that you should systematize any process in your business that is performed frequently, and that, if completed in a predictable, consistent manner, would increase the value and profits of your business.

Judging whether your systematization efforts are working or not should be very easy. First, you should notice your employees making fewer mistakes. If not, more systems are clearly needed.

Second, you should find yourself with more free time because your systematization efforts eliminated your daily fire-fighting tasks—your employees now know what to do and how to resolve problems.

Third, if your systematization efforts are working, you should start seeing improved revenues and profits.

I once worked with a client to systematize how he launched new products to his customers. Previously, the process of selling a new product took too long and was marred with mistakes. For example, developing the sales collateral required rounds of revisions and he had to check for typos and errors that should have been caught before his review. He often had to remind his website developer to add the new product to his website, and this pushed back the launch date. He typically had to be the one to prepare the customer service team to answer calls about the new product.

After the process was fully systematized, his team simply followed the process maps and SOPs for introducing a new product. The right people touched the project at the right times. Action items were methodically completed and checked off the to-do list. Products were introduced more quickly and generated more sales than before because the process was executed flawlessly. The best part was, while all this was going on, my client was able to spend his time developing the next product that would boost his company's sales and profits even further.

In the next few chapters we will develop a detailed marketing plan. You will learn about a key new marketing metric to judge your performance and how to methodically improve your performance so you can dominate your market.

CHAPTER 7

HOW TO OUT-MARKET YOUR MARKET

When you developed your vision in earlier chapters, you (hopefully) documented lofty sales and profit goals. You also became aware that to achieve such results, you must reverse engineer your financial metrics and business assets as discussed in previous chapters.

It also requires you to incorporate world-class marketing into your strategic plan. Even if you've built the best product, developed a highly trained team, and created amazing systems, if you aren't able to reach or convince customers to buy, you will not achieve success. The good news is that despite what you might assume, world-class marketing does NOT necessitate the type of marketing that Fortune 500 companies with big budgets use. Rather, there are extremely low-cost techniques that allow you to fully leverage every marketing effort you take, thereby increasing your revenues and profits exponentially.

To implement world-class marketing in your business, you need to (1) understand your true marketing goal and (2) build the strongest marketing system in your industry. This chapter will show you how to do both so you can grow your sales and profits and dominate your market.

The Most Important Number in Your Business

To understand your true marketing goal, you need to understand the most important number in your business. That number is *profit per impression* (PPI). This is the amount of profit you generate from everyone who hears about your company.

Let me give you an example. Say your competitor runs an ad (for a $500 widget radio, TV, print, etc.), to which 1 percent of people responded by calling the company. Out of that 1 percent, your competitor was able to convert 35 percent into customers. The average purchaser bought 1.5 widgets. Let's assume your competitor's profit margin on each widget is 30 percent. Finally, your competitor has little customer follow-up, so we expect that only 10 percent of customers will repurchase from it.

Here's a summary of your competitor's KPIs:

- 1 percent response rate
- 35 percent conversion rate
- $500 price per widget
- 1.5 widgets per buyer
- 30 percent profit margin
- 10 percent repurchase rate

Assuming the ad reached 10,000 target customers, your competitor's gross profit from the ad would have been $8,662.50 (minus the cost of the ad).

Now let's assume that your company did a 20 percent better job on each KPI than your competitor, except that you still charged the same $500 per widget. So your KPIs would be:

- 1.2 percent response rate
- 42 percent conversion rate

- $500 price per widget
- 1.8 widgets per buyer
- 36 percent profit margin
- 12 percent repurchase rate

If your ad reached the same 10,000 target customers, these KPIs would make your gross profit $19,596—2.3 times greater than your competitor's.

What would happen if you generated 2.3 times greater profits per impression than your competitors? You would absolutely *dominate* them. You would advertise them out of the market. You'd be able to advertise in places where they couldn't. For example, they never could have purchased an ad space that cost $10,000 because they only generated $8,662 in gross profits from it. But you could pay for that ad all day long.

How do you get 20 percent higher PPI KPIs than your competitors? You do this by keeping the following crucial metrics in mind and methodically improving your performance on each. Let's look at each one in more detail.

Response Rate

The first metric in which you beat your competitor was response rate, or the percentage of people who heard/read/saw your ad and contacted you. How do you improve this rate?

There are a few answers. First, the more you know about your customers' wants and needs, the more easily you can design an advertisement that appeals to them. And the more you know about them, the better you could craft a unique selling proposition (USP) to attracted them.

For example, if you are local hardware company and you know your typical buyer is a busy male with a wife, kids, and dog, you could easily craft ads with a higher response rate. For example, an ad with the headline "Hey, busy dad, we have the tools to help you get your home repairs done more quickly and inexpensively" would better appeal to your customer. Add imagery in the advertisement of a dad with his wife, kids, and dog in the yard and you would increase response rates further by better identifying with your target customers.

You could also boost response rate by developing better offers that attract customers, such as an offer for a 90-day money-back guarantee.

Conversion Rate

The next metric on which you beat your competitor is conversion rates, or the percentage of prospective customers that you *converted* into actual customers. A few ways you could do this include having a better process in place for training your staff and sales team, providing better employee incentives (e.g., commissions or bonuses for closing sales), or by developing and testing sales scripts that boost results.

Number of Widgets Per Buyer

The next metric on which you outperformed competitors is the amount of their initial purchase. To increase this metric, you could convince buyers to purchase more widgets, or upsell them on related items, such as products that allow them to get more value from their widget or that complete the job the widget performs more quickly. In either case, customers would have paid you more money per sale. As with conversion rates, you can achieve this through better hiring, training, and so on.

Profit Margin

Better systematizing your business and implementing the right processes and procedures would allow you to generate higher profits per sale than your competitors. For example, if you create tighter systems and procedures for fulfilling customer orders as discussed in the last chapter, your team would perform at a lower cost than competitors.

Repurchase Rate

The final metric where you beat competitors was the repurchase rate, which is your customer lifetime value. By doing a better job of communicating with your clients and showing them how special they are, you could get them to buy from you again. This would give you a massive competitive advantage.

YOUR MARKETING SYSTEM

Improving your performance on each of these metrics provides a way for you to dominate—*really* dominate—your competitors. And the best way to accomplish this is to look at marketing as a system and methodically improve each and every component of the system.

Your marketing system includes all the processes your company employs, from attracting customers to gaining repeat purchases from them. Specifically, the four aspects of your marketing system are:

1. Lead generation
2. Conversion rates
3. Transaction prices/average purchase amount
4. Lifetime customer value/number of purchases

Even if your marketing seems effective, by developing, tracking, and improving each aspect of your marketing system you will realize tremendous gains in sales and profits.

In the following section I will show you how to optimize your lead generation so you gain many new customers who are interested in purchasing your products and services. In the next chapter I will walk you through the other three aspects of your marketing system so you can turn these leads into lifelong customers.

HOW TO OPTIMIZE LEAD GENERATION

Lead generation includes all the ways your company prompts potential customers to call or contact you, visit your website, or visit your physical store. There are a variety of lead generation tactics you can use to increase the number of leads your company receives, such as direct mail, newspaper, and radio advertising; customer referral programs; joint ventures; holding educational seminars; telemarketing; and so on.

Knowing which techniques work best for you and how to execute on them allows successful entrepreneurs and business owners to generate a nearly endless flow of new leads. The key is to continuously:

1. Improve your success with your current lead generation tactics, and
2. Test and add new lead generation sources

Although the first comes easily to many people, most entrepreneurs and business owners fail miserably with the second. They stick with the one or two lead generation sources that are currently working for them and don't employ anything new.

Simply sticking with what works is too risky a strategy. What if, for example, your primary method of generating leads is newspaper advertising in a newspaper that goes out of business? What if a particular publication signs an exclusive deal with one of your competitors or raises its rates significantly? What if, and this will hit close to home for many local retail businesses, customers stop using the Yellow Pages, where you've been exclusively advertising for years?

In any of those cases, you lose, which is why it is vital to diversify your lead sources. Even if your new lead sources are not as profitable as your existing ones, you should employ them as long as they are profitable (or can be, after testing and tweaking).

Improving each aspect of your marketing system should make a myriad of lead sources profitable for your business. Another thing to remember is that many of these sources would be unprofitable for your competitors, which allows you to grow as they wither away.

The following list shows some of the top lead generation sources (also known as media sources or marketing channels) you should be using or testing for your business:

1. *Direct Mail.* Direct mail is precisely what the name says it is: Sending pieces of mail (postcards, letters, etc.) directly to your target customers. Sending the right pieces to the right customers can be extremely profitable for most companies.

2. *Print Ads.* Print ads in the right newspapers, magazines, or trade journals can effectively reach your desired customers.

3. *Radio and TV Ads.* Radio and television ads are actually much less expensive than most business owners

think—particularly cable television ads, which can be used to target specific customer segments based on the networks or programs your target market tends to watch.

4. *Networking.* There are generally numerous opportunities to meet prospective customers at local, industry, and discipline (e.g., marketing, finance, etc.) events. If this category is applicable for your business, consider getting a trade show booth to capture leads.

5. *Telemarketing.* Although the National Do Not Call Registry list might apply to some or many of your customers, telemarketing remains a viable marketing method for most businesses. Like direct mail, it allows you to precisely target customers.

6. *Event Marketing.* Hosting your own events is a great way to garner publicity and bring tons of prospective customers to you. The more people who attend your event, the more social proof you will generate. In others words, people see others around you (e.g., buying your product, visiting your store, etc.) and become more comfortable doing those actions themselves.

7. *E-mail and Print Newsletter Marketing.* E-mail marketing, which can include e-newsletters or periodic e-mails, is a great way to communicate with current and prospective customers, as are print newsletters. Both methods allow you to contact your customers frequently, which is crucial in getting them to buy from you.

8. *Press Releases/PR.* PR is a highly cost-effective way for entrepreneurs and business owners to reach their target customers. It has the additional benefit of credibility; not only do prospective customers become aware of you, if you are mentioned in a major news source, they see you in a more favorable light.

9. *Online Marketing (SEO and Search Engine Marketing [SEM])*. A good SEO strategy can get your company to appear in the top results of search engines (such as Google) when a customer searches for one of your target keywords. SEM includes paying to appear at the top of these searches and in other webpages your customers frequent. Both tactics allow you to effectively reach your target customers.

10. *Social Media Marketing*. Social media websites such as Twitter, LinkedIn, Facebook, and YouTube allow you to create relationships, buzz, and loyal followings among your customers as well as run contests and build brand awareness, which will help drive traffic and sales.

11. *Partnerships*. Having the right partners can help generate a great deal of leads for your business. The ideal partner is a company that serves the same client that you serve with a noncompetitive product or service. For example, if you offer air duct cleaning services, forming partnerships with house cleaning/maid services that clean homes, but not air ducts would be a great way to get introductions to ideal potential customers (ones that are already paying to keep their homes clean).

Although this is clearly not a comprehensive list of lead generation sources, they are the sources with which I and my clients have had the most success. Virtually all of these sources can be used in all industries. Importantly, few to no companies use all 11 of them. Take a moment to decide which of the 11 sources that you are not currently using might work best for you. In doing this assessment, consider starting with the lead generation sources that:

- You or a team member have used successfully in the past (perhaps at another job) and thus have some experience with

- You have seen working for a competitor or noncompetitor serving a similar customer base as yours
- Intuitively seem like they should work

Then add testing this new lead generation source to your goals for your next quarter. As you might have guessed, building profitable lead generation sources is a key business asset that will lead you toward your end vision.

How to Get the Most out of Your Marketing Efforts

You need to target the right customer and understand their needs to effectively choose your marketing channels or media sources. For example, social media marketing might not be the best choice if you have elderly clients because they are less prone to use Facebook or Twitter. Therefore, you need to start with a comprehensive understanding of (1) who your target customers are and (2) what their wants and needs are when developing your marketing plan.

Let's say you're selling a teeth whitening product and you know your target customers are men ages 30 to 40, making between $40,000 and $50,000 per year, living in Manhattan, and who own dogs. You could effectively reach this market via several of the marketing channels listed previously and speak to their exact needs. For example, with research and testing, you could find the websites that best cater to this segment, the radio shows they listen to, and the television shows they watch. You could buy lists of men fitting these characteristics and target them (if you search, you can create a list of men of a certain age and income level who have purchased teeth whitening products).

This would yield you an enormous ROI on your marketing efforts. Unfortunately, most businesses don't take the time to create this profile, and thus waste money targeting the wrong audience with their marketing messages.

It is also crucial to remember the 80/20 rule when you create your customer profile: 20 percent of your customers will generate 80 percent of your revenue. Not everyone who buys from you will fall neatly into the detailed description of your target customer, and that's ok. If you focus on marketing to and serving your core customer, you'll get more of the 20 percent you want and thus much more bang for your marketing buck.

You can think about your customer profile as a bell curve, as shown in Figure 7.1. You create your customer profile directed at the person who falls directly in the center of your curve. This person is your ideal prospect and you serve them perfectly.

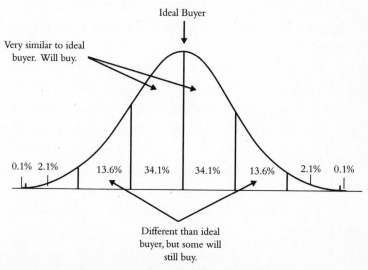

Figure 7.1 Customer Bell Curve

Even people who are slightly different than your ideal buyer will purchase, as visualized by the area one standard deviation away from the ideal person on both sides of center. Even people two standard deviations away can and will buy, but not with the frequency and concentration of people aligning more closely with the ideal person.

For example, fast food chains such as McDonald's and Burger King primarily target teenagers with their advertisements. However, these same ads attract customers of all age groups.

The following are some questions that will allow you to better understand the customer needs that your products or services fill so you can better identify your target market.

1. What needs, wants, or desires does your offering satisfy, or what problems does your product or service solve (e.g., cleanliness, exclusivity, results, safety, timeliness, convenience, atmosphere)?
2. How much do your products or services cost? (Are you going after the mass market? Do you offer a luxury good?)
3. Who is the customer decision maker who chooses whether to buy your products or services? Is there also a customer influencer (e.g., kids influencing mom to buy a toy)?
4. How do customers purchase your products? (For example, website or retail store? If a retail store, the target customer will need to live within a certain geographic area.)

The next thing to do is to examine your target customers' demographic profile by finding out:

- Where do they live or work?
- How old are they?

- What is their income?
- What gender(s) are they?
- What nationality or ethnicity?
- What is their average household size?
- In what occupations do they work?
- What language(s) do they speak?

If you are serving business customers:

- What is their company revenue?
- What industry are they in?
- What is their job function or title?
- To whom do they report?

Finally, you should examine your target customers' psychographic profile. *Psychographics* is the study and classification of people according to their attitudes, aspirations, and other psychological criteria. By getting a handle on this, you'll be better able to attract and convert them into becoming customers. You can get an idea by asking:

- What activities do your customers enjoy?
- What interests do they have?
- What are their strongest opinions?
- What attitudes do they have?
- What do they believe in?
- What are their core values?

Based on your answers to these questions, you must develop and document your detailed customer profile.

Go to www.startatend.com to download a worksheet to define your detailed customer profile.

Once you have a detailed profile of your ideal customer, you can reach prospective customers a lot more easily. Clearly, if you know where they live and work, what they like, and what media they watch, listen to, or read, you can choose the best lead generation sources to reach them. You can also craft advertisements that better appeal to their specific needs, wants, and interests. Effective marketers understand and leverage this. For example, when I pick up my wife's *Vogue* magazine, I'll often read an advertisement and won't get the point of it. Why? Because I'm nowhere close to being their ideal customer target. Conversely, my wife might see that same advertisement and think, "I must buy this!"

This example and the questions discussed previously should help you understand fully the incredible value of knowing as much as possible about target customers. However, in many cases, you may have just guessed at the previous questions. For example, you may not really know their occupations or interests. If that's true, there's a simple solution: survey them. The purpose of the survey is to (1) confirm your target customer definition and (2) determine how to attract more target customers.

The easiest way to conduct a survey is to use a free online survey tool or a simple-to-complete, single-page questionnaire to gather information by asking the following:

1. Questions to *confirm your target customer definition*:
   - What is your ZIP code? (To find location)
   - What are the key reasons why you purchased our product/service? (List several reasons and have customers check all the reasons that apply; also put an *other* category with space for the respondent to write their answers)
   - Which of the following activities do you do? (Once again, list several and have an *other* category)

2. Questions to determine how to *attract more target customers*:
- What television shows do you watch?
- What magazines do you read?
- How did you find out about us?

This set of questions will tell you how to find more target customers. For example, if a large percentage of your customers read *Better Homes & Gardens* or *Forbes* magazine, then advertising in those magazines would probably yield a great ROI. Likewise, if many of your customers found out about you through an event you sponsored, you would want to sponsor similar events in the future.

You should now understand the concept of a marketing system and how improving each piece of the system can boost your sales and profits. You also learned the importance of understanding who your ideal customers are, how to better define these customers, and how you can leverage this information by choosing the perfect lead generation sources. Finally, you learned the 11 most effective lead generation sources and how you must continue to test new sources to eliminate risk and gain competitive advantage.

In the next chapter we will discuss the final three pieces of your marketing system. You will learn how to increase the percentage of your leads who become customers, drive customers to spend more with your company than they currently do, and lock up, or keep, your customers for life.

CHAPTER 8

SECURING AND LOCKING UP YOUR CUSTOMERS

In the last chapter, I introduced you to the concept of the marketing system, and to the fact that you can dominate your market by methodically improving each of the four aspects of the system. We covered in detail the first part of the system—lead generation.

Now that you know how to generate more leads, you need to improve the final three parts of your system: (1) increasing conversion rates, (2) increasing transaction prices, and (3) increasing the lifetime value of your customers.

Each of these three marketing system components will significantly boost your company's sales and profits. But the last one, increasing the lifetime value of your customers, has the added benefit of making your business nearly bulletproof. For instance, I recently worked with an entrepreneur who took his business to $10 million in sales only to have it collapse when the economy experienced a downturn. If he had focused on improving lifetime customer value, he would have built a loyal customer base in that business. When the economic downturn occurred, he would have lost some sales. But the majority of his loyal customer base would have continued buying from him.

His business would have survived and been poised for significant growth when the economy rebounded.

This chapter shows you how to improve the final three aspects of your marketing system and presents two additional marketing tactics that will make your competitors wish they had chosen a different business.

HOW TO OPTIMIZE CONVERSION RATES

You learned in the last chapter how to better attract leads to your business. The next part of your marketing system to strengthen is your ability to convert these leads into paying customers. This percentage—the number of customers divided by the number of leads—is known as your *conversion rate*.

Increasing your conversion rates can dramatically increase your profits because your biggest marketing costs are typically used in lead generation. Consider this example:

Number of Prospective Customers	10,000	10,000
Conversion Rate	**10 percent**	**12 percent**
Number of Sales	1,000	1,200
Profit per Sale	$200	$200
Total Profit	$200,000	$240,000

You can see here that increasing the conversion rate by just 2 percent increased profits by $40,000.

In the following section you will learn the six strategies to use to increase your conversion rates. After you review each one, consider and describe how you will employ them in your business.

1. Strengthen Your USP

I recently spoke at a large trade show for business owners. Because I arrived before I was scheduled to speak, I spent a few minutes walking the exhibit floor and checking out the booths.

Most booths were extremely boring. They had fancy displays with the company name, but I couldn't clearly tell what they did or why I should care about them. Two booths, on both sides of the boring versus exciting spectrum, caught my attention.

As I walked by the first booth, the representative stopped me and said, "Do you have 30 seconds to see something really cool?" Although I had no idea what his business was about, this pitch was unique and I was intrigued. I gave him 30 seconds of my time. In fact, because his 30-second pitch was cool, I ended up speaking with him for 5 minutes.

The second booth that caught my attention was on the other side of the spectrum. It was a web development company, and it caught my attention because the headline on its display was so bad. The headline read, "The leader in customized website solutions." Why did I find this so bad? It showed nothing unique about the business. Is the company faster than its competition? Cheaper? Does it guarantee better results? Does it focus specifically on helping businesses like mine? The answer to all of these questions is "I don't know," and that's why the booth was empty.

I later did a Google search on the phrase, "the leader in customized website solutions." Google came back with 32,700,000 results, telling me that the headline is far from unique. And because of that, neither I nor the other business owners at the event noticed this poorly marketed company. What this company needed was a strong unique selling proposition (USP).

A strong USP is one of the most important elements of your marketing plan because your USP separates your product or service from your competitors'. Your USP defines what makes your product or service a unique, must-have item. A great USP will lower your cost of getting leads and increase your conversion rates.

In fact, great USPs have been noted as the keys to success for companies in multiple industries, including:

- The Domino's Pizza USP—"Fresh hot pizza delivered to your door in thirty minutes or less, guaranteed" (key USP elements are quality [hot/fresh] and timeliness [30 minutes or less])
- The FedEx USP—"When it absolutely, positively has to be there overnight." (key USP elements are reliability and quick delivery)

A few more famous examples:

- Head & Shoulders: You get rid of dandruff
- Olay: Younger-looking skin
- M&M's: Melts in your mouth, not in your hand
- Wonder Bread: Wonder Bread helps build strong bodies 12 ways
- Nyquil: The nighttime, sniffling, sneezing, coughing, aching, stuffy head, fever, so-you-can-rest medicine

And it's not just big name brands that use these effectively. Here are some more USP examples used by local businesses:

- We are the only jewelry repair shop that will buy your jewelry if you are not 100 percent satisfied with our work.
- Chinese food delivered in 30 minutes or we'll pay for it!
- No other desk company will pay for your shipping.
- Our clam chowder recipe is so secret, only seven people in the world know it!

- We guarantee you will have a comfortable experience and never have to wait more than 15 minutes for the dentist or you'll receive a free exam.

The following is a series of questions and exercises to create or improve your own business's USP.

1. Describe the *key values and benefits* your customers receive from buying your products or services.
2. Describe *how customers feel* after using your product or service (e.g., their teeth will be whiter, they will feel more confident, they will feel safer, they will have more energy, they will have more money, etc.).
3. Describe *how your company is different* and stands out from competitors (factors such as price, location, exclusivity, results, safety, timeliness, etc.). (If nothing makes you unique currently, come up with some new ideas!)
4. Describe *how you would like customers to think about your business* (e.g., as being the guaranteed lowest cost provider, as being the most reliable company, etc.).
5. Combine your answers to these questions to create a paragraph that describes your USP.
6. Condense your USP summary into just one line. Use the Domino's and FedEx examples as inspiration. Realize that although you can't say everything in just one line, you must get your key points across in a manner that people will easily remember.

Improving your USP will cause customers to identify more closely with your products and services and see them as the ideal solutions to their needs. As a result, your USP will increase your response and conversion rates.

2. Improve Your Offers

The second strategy to increase your conversion rates is to craft *powerful offers*, or special deals that you promote to customers to make your product or services irresistible to them. Good offers will bring you more new customers and bring previous customers back.

Consider whether one or several of the following five basic types of offers might work for your company.

1. Free Offers and Free Trials

A free offer could include a free information piece (e.g., a special report), or it could be a free trial of your product or service.

By giving something of value away for free, you encourage prospective customers to try your product or service, which can influence them to become paying customers.

Some examples of free offers and free trials are:

- A report on how to choose the right piano for your family (used by retail piano companies to attract leads and close customers)
- Trials/testers of perfume at department stores
- A 7- to 30-day trial gym membership

Such offers encourage prospective clients to take action and eliminate the friction or barrier to completing the sale caused by requiring payment. In the gym membership example, customers may be unsure whether the gym is right for them. The required initial month's payment causes additional friction, which stops customers from completing the purchase.

Offering the free trial removes this friction. It makes it easier for prospective customers to take action because they don't need to take any financial risk. And in many cases, after experiencing the free trial, the prospects will see the value in the product or service and become paying customers.

2. Guarantee Offers

Guarantees give customers the confidence that your product or service will meet their needs. They are often referred to as risk reversal because they put the risk of customer dissatisfaction on you and not the customer, which results in more customer purchases.

Some guarantee offers include money-back guarantees for a specific time period (e.g., 30-day, 60-day, 1-year, or even lifetime money-back guarantees). Note that the longer your guarantee period, the higher your sales usually are. In fact, for one of my popular products, I noticed an increased conversion rate when I changed the guarantee period from 30 to 365 days (although the vast majority of actual refunds still take place within 30 days). You can also use double-your-money-back guarantees if feasible for your business because they should increase customer conversions even further.

A few examples that run the gamut of price ranges are:

- New carpet retailer guarantees that any stains will be removed for free (or the carpet replaced) for one year
- Guaranteed lowest interest rate on a car loan
- Guaranteed satisfaction on a candy bar or your money back

3. Packaged Offers

A packaged offer combines multiple products into a package that best suits the needs of your customers.

Examples range from McDonald's Happy Meals to starter kits that offer each of the products a beginner needs to embark on something (e.g., a baseball starter kit may include a helmet, batting glove, bat, and baseballs). Providing your customers with a packaged offer creates a strong perception of value in the customers' eyes and allows you to make a nice profit on the sale.

4. Discount Offers

Discount offers give customers products or services at reduced fees. And they certainly work. Recently, I received a postcard in the mail from a local company offering me a 25 percent discount on installing an electric fence. Not only was this great targeting (they must have purchased a list showing that I fit a certain demographic profile and had recently purchased a dog), but the discount caused me to take action. I had been thinking about an electric fence for a while, but I was never fully prompted to take action. I had seen advertisements in the past, but it wasn't until I saw this discount offer that I took action. Customers like feeling they are getting a good value for their money, which makes discounts very effective.

5. Premium Offers

Premium offers are when you give something away for free to customers who make a purchase. They are often a better strategy than discount offers because you receive a higher payment. In premium offers, you leave your prices the same but offer more value. In my electric fence example, the seller could have left the price of the fence the same and added "includes two free hours of dog training worth $199" as the premium or incentive to get me to buy. If they had, I would have made the purchase and paid the company more money (remember, I paid them the full price minus my 25 percent discount).

Other examples of premium offers include:

- Buy one hot dog, get one free
- Buy a computer today and get 25 percent off on any software packages we sell

- Buy a subscription to our magazine today and get a free t-shirt or bag
- Buy our DVD series and get one year of free online access to our additional videos

6. Getting Customer to Take Action Now

The final piece of a great offer is that it influences customers to act (i.e., to buy your product or service) right away. Ideas to incorporate into your offer to get customers to act now include:

- Limited-time offers (offer only good through Saturday at midnight)
- Limited-availability offers (we only have 45 left in stock!)
- Fast-action bonuses (the first 50 buyers will get these extra bonuses)

As you might imagine, by combining two or more types of the offers just listed you can create an extremely compelling offer. For example, had a *different* dog fencing company offered me a 25 percent discounted price on fencing, added dog training as a premium offer, given me a one-year satisfaction guarantee, and said the offer ended in three days, you could bet I would have called and purchased their offer right away.

3. Improve Your Sales Scripts

The third strategy to increase your conversion rates is to improve your sales scripts.

Whether you know it or not, most successful businesses have these. Scripts can be as simple as a restaurant such as McDonald's saying, "Would you like fries with that?" or "Would you like to supersize that?" These simple questions result in millions of dollars of increased profits each year.

You can begin creating the most effective scripts for your-self and your staff by citing all the objections you typically hear from prospective customers. You want to be able to address these objections *before* customers do to increase conversions. For example, if your prospective customers often complain (and don't buy) because your prices are too high, you need a script to address this. You could have your sales team say the follow-ing within all sales conversations, "Let me stop you right there. I think I know what you're thinking right now. That our prices are a little high, right? Well, you know, many of our 5,000 other satisfied clients thought that too when they first came to us. But then, after buying from us, they have repeatedly come back and told us that we were worth the extra money, and that they expe-rienced greater satisfaction and had significantly fewer problems than when they tried the lower cost and quality solutions our competitors offer."

Then you should train your team on how to use the sales scripts (e.g., conduct mock sales training), and be sure to track the results of your scripts. This will allow you to determine which scripts work best and modify your scripts to improve results.

Finally, you might want to consider creating sales quotas, commissions, or bonuses for employees who convert the most prospects to customers using the sales scripts.

4. Increase Your Social Proof

The fourth strategy to increase your conversion rates is to improve your *social proof*. Social proof is a psychological response that makes us want to do something other people are doing. For example, if you're in a town you've never been to and see two restaurants, one that's crowded and the other that's completely empty, you'll be more prone to choose the one that's crowded. Customers are more comfortable buying when there is social proof because it gives an indication that other customers have been satisfied with your product and service before. Few people want to take their chances on an unproven product, particularly in a competitive environment.

Two effective ways to show social proof are customer testimonials and news clippings. We see examples of this every day, from the restaurant that has framed and proudly promotes its newspaper reviews to the back of most business books showing quotations from other prominent writers and business leaders about how great the book is to the dry cleaner who posts signed pictures of all the celebrities it has served.

The point is this: If you get any press, collect it. Mention it on your website. Post it in your store. Include it in your brochures. Gather as many testimonials as you can get. Depending on your needs, testimonials can be in print, audio, or video format. Whatever you do, make sure your prospective customers see these testimonials because they will increase interest in buying from you.

Let me give you a final example of the importance of social proof. I recently spoke at large event in which attendees could choose from several seminars. About 15 minutes into my presentation, two women entered the room to hear me speak. At the time, about 100 other people were seated and listening to me. I stopped the presentation and asked the women, "If you walked into this room and saw that only three people were sitting here listening to me, would you still have come inside?" Both their answers were a definitive no.

5. Nurture and Never Give Up

The fifth strategy to increase your conversion rates is to nurture prospective clients and never give up. It is often the case that a customer is genuinely interested in buying a product or service from you, but doesn't because of timing or other issues. Maybe they had a temporary financial setback like a car repair they weren't expecting and they need to put the decision on hold. Maybe they feel it's an important decision and a big purchase and want to spend a few weeks researching it.

Most businesses make the mistake of giving up when they don't make the sale immediately. Smart businesses, however, nurture their prospective customers. The easiest way to do this is via e-mail. Collect your prospective customers' e-mail addresses and set up an autoresponder that e-mails them regularly— perhaps once every three days for four months. These e-mails can give the prospective customer quality information on the product or service they are seeking while positioning you and your company's products or services as the best choice. Staying fresh in the customer's mind and being a highly knowledgeable resource will both dramatically increase your conversion rates.

Don't give up when you lose a sale. Rather, contact the prospect periodically thereafter (a week later, a month later, etc.) and try again. Use your second try to give the prospect a special offer and a reason why. For example, you could say that you just got new capacity and can now offer the same service that you proposed at a 25 percent discount. Maybe a new product came in and you can sell it at the same price as the now old and inferior product you previously pitched.

You get the point: Don't give up. Whether via e-mail, direct mail, or telephone, you want to constantly interact with your prospects. Of course, the same is true with your current and past customers. The more you stay fresh in your customers' mind, the more they will return and buy from you.

Before we move on, let me give you an example of the power of nurturing. On my company Growthink's website, we offer several free reports that require a person to register by submitting their e-mail address. Once they register, we e-mail them the report, send a series of e-mails, and add them to our newsletter list. When I looked at the history of some of our recent clients, I noticed that several of them had first come to our website and downloaded a report two or three years ago. That's right—these clients required two or three years and hundreds of e-mails to decide the timing was right and that Growthink was the right firm with whom they should work. I'm sure these clients also visited the websites of my competitors two or three years prior. But only my company nurtured them, and thus reaped the rewards.

6. Improve Prospective Customers' Perceptions of You

The sixth and final strategy to increase your conversion rates is to improve prospective customers' perceptions of you because how customers perceive you will influence whether they want to do business with you.

It is vital that your brand positioning is consistent with how customers view you when they're in your presence. For example, if you are promoting your company as a premium service provider, how does your staff look? Are they dressed sloppily? Are they well-spoken? What about your showroom? Is it clean and easy to navigate? Are your product displays new? You can easily increase your customer conversions by creating an image of quality that supports your desired brand positioning.

For instance, at Saks Fifth Avenue, you'll see the upscale image the retailer is trying to portray in many ways. Store sections are meticulously cleaned, lighted, and displayed elegantly. You won't see workers wearing denim or flip-flops (unless they work in the denim section, of course).

These six strategies will allow you to turn more prospective customers into paying customers, significantly increasing your sales and profits in the process. In the following section you will learn tactics for increasing the prices these customers pay each time they buy from you.

HOW TO OPTIMIZE TRANSACTION PRICES

Your marketing system will continue to get stronger as you learn how to attract leads more effectively and turn those leads into customers. The next part of improving your system is to get customers to pay *more* each time they buy from you because doing so will maximize your revenues and profits. We call this strategy *increasing your transaction prices or average purchase amount*, and there are four core methods for achieving this. Each one is described in detail in the following sections.

1. Raising Prices

This is the simplest tactic for increasing your average transaction price. It's no surprise that most companies are hesitant to raise prices out of fear they will lose prospects and clients to their competitors. However, studies have shown that price is often a secondary factor in customer buying decisions. If customers and prospective customers like other factors about you, your products, and your services, they are often willing to pay higher prices than you might initially assume.

If you are competing in a very price-sensitive market, try to get your prospective customers to compare apples with oranges. That is, position yourself in a way that emphasizes the difference between you and your competitors by explaining your superior service, which will allow you to command a higher price.

When considering raising prices, ask yourself these questions:

- For which products or services can you possibly raise prices?
- How much will you raise the price?
- How will you test to see whether the new price raises profits? (For example, after competitor Netflix raised prices, movie rental kiosk company Redbox started testing increasing its prices in kiosks in select cities.)
- What can you do to position yourself differently to outsell competitors even at higher prices?

2. Offering Product or Service Packages

Another tactic is to provide product or service packages that include multiple offerings that best suit your customers' needs. For example, when my daughter wanted to take up painting, I bought her a painting kit that included paints, brushes, canvases, and a paint tray palette. I chose this option over buying the items individually, rewarding the company who had the insight to create such a package. Service company examples include a car wash that offers a basic outside car wash and an expanded car wash that also includes interior detailing, and so on.

Offering a package such as this creates a perception of value in the customers' eyes while increasing the transaction price on the sale. If you're trying to discern what kind of product or service packages you might be able to offer, consider these questions:

- What individual products or services are customers already buying together? In the painting kit example, it is obvious that customers who purchase paints also purchase brushes and canvases. In fact, if you sell consumer products, one easy way to identify additional products your customers purchase is to visit Amazon.com. Find the product you sell, and then look in the section titled "Customers Who Bought This Item Also Bought" to find such products. What if you don't sell consumer products? There's still an easy way to find out what else your customers buy—ask them!

- How might you package your product or service offerings to better meet your customers' full needs? In the case of my daughter's painting, her full need was to acquire all the painting products required to perform the task (brushes, paints, etc.) and to learn how to paint. As such, I would have paid even more for a package that also included education on how to become a better painter, perhaps a DVD or a workbook.

3. Upselling and Cross-Selling

Usually, customers are buying your product or service to solve a problem or fulfill a need. If you explain it to them effectively, they'll typically realize that purchasing additional products or services can help them better meet that need. For example, if a prospective customer is about to buy a $12 hammer from you, you may be able to upsell the $20 hammer that reduces the chance for blisters or other injuries. You also may be able to cross-sell to the customer. For instance, if you discover that the customer needs the hammer to do a certain project, you may be able to sell nails and other supplies that will help accomplish that project. This allows you to meet the customer's needs more completely while making more money—a true win-win!

Consider these questions when trying to determine upselling and cross-selling opportunities:

- Currently, what are your top-selling products or services?
- What products or services could be upsold or cross-sold for each to fully meet customer needs?

Recently, when purchasing a new car for my wife, I found that most automobile manufacturers and dealers do this extremely effectively. They offer several à la carte upgrade options as well as upgrade packages, such as the "touring" package that includes several upgrades. Most also cross-sell, offering items such as window etchings to prevent theft, deer deterrence devices (which send out signals to deter deer from coming near), and insurance products.

Don't be afraid to offer more than one upsell or cross-sell because every customer's precise needs and wants may differ. Some customers may purchase more than one upsell. Consider airline companies. The last time I purchased a seat, I was upsold on paying for luggage, paying for seats with extra legroom, paying for flight insurance, paying for in-flight movies and food, and even paying for the convenience of boarding the plane earlier.

Most companies wait to improve their marketing systems until it's absolutely essential. For example, airlines could have upsold customers on more legroom and priority boarding years ago, but they only started doing so recently when they absolutely needed the extra profits to stay in business. Imagine they had made such changes years ago; they would have enjoyed much more success. Don't make the same mistake. Rather, proactively leverage all the ideas you are learning in this book and start dominating your market today.

4. Increasing the Order Size

The McDonald's "Would you like to supersize that?" question is a great example of growing transaction prices by increasing order sizes. This simple question has buyers paying more for more of the fast food chain's products at a much greater amount than the increased cost of the product provided. In fact, it's been suggested that this one line, when first introduced, doubled the company's profits overnight.

Any time you have a customer buying anything, there is usually an opportunity to have them purchase more of whatever they're buying. You might consider offering a discount to influence the larger purchase, such as buy one, get one at half price. Whatever the specific terms, you can use these questions to determine how to get customers to buy more from you during each transaction:

- Currently, what are your top selling products or services?
- Currently, what is the average amount purchased by your customers?
- How could customers be better off or more satisfied by purchasing a larger amount of that product or service?
- Will you need to offer an incentive, such as a bulk discount or premium (e.g., buy three and we'll include unlimited telephone support) to gain the larger order?

One concern business owners sometimes have is whether by offering a larger order size now, they will lose out on future revenues. For example, let's say you are a manufacturer and have a customer who wants to purchase a one-month supply of your widgets. Let's say that instead, you convince the customer to purchase a six-month supply at a 10 percent discount.

You might think that if you continued to charge the customer monthly, you would have received a 10 percent higher payment. However, there are two flaws to this thinking. First, there is the time value of money, and having more payment now is more valuable than having it later. Second, and often more important, unless you have contractual agreements with customers obligating them to purchase only from you, you have no guarantee they will continue buying from you. In fact, if you hadn't given them the six-month supply deal, in months two, three, four, five, and six, they might have purchased from your competition.

Increasing customer transaction prices directly increase your sales and profits. Don't think about increasing transaction prices as taking advantage of your customers. You're not. Rather, you are better satisfying their needs. Likewise, don't think your customers will be offended when you offer cross-sell, upsell, and increased order size opportunities. Have you ever seen someone storm out of McDonald's in disgust, saying, "The nerve of that employee; I can't believe she asked if I wanted fries with that!"? If customers don't want what you're offering, they'll simply say no.

The next section presents the fourth and final piece of the marketing system: increasing the lifetime value of your customers.

How to Optimize Lifetime Customer Value

In addition to the various ways you've learned to further satisfy your customers, there's one more thing you can do if you want to really dominate your competition. Fortunately for you, this last piece will boost your profits even further.

It involves optimizing the lifetime value of your customers by getting them to make more purchases from you over time. All too often, entrepreneurs and business owners get so caught up in the initial customer sale that they fail to generate as much long-term revenues from their customers as they could. *Successful* entrepreneurs and business owners get customers to buy again by employing the three techniques you will learn in the following text. Not only will these methods boost your revenues and profits, they will allow you to develop ongoing, predictable, and growing revenue streams, which is the key to both successfully growing *and* exiting a company.

1. Ongoing Communications

This is simply contacting your customers often with the goal of increasing the frequency with which customers order from you. Seems easy enough, right? However, 99 percent of companies fail to do this. For example, how often do you hear from your dentist? I hear from my dentist twice per year—when I'm scheduled for my cleanings. If my dentist contacted me 12 times per year, she could sell me on additional services such as teeth whitening or on products such as electric toothbrushes. She might even get me to refer my friends. I'm not quite sure why she doesn't; after all, she has my address.

Ongoing communications with customers can take many forms, all of which fall into the category of direct marketing— that which you deliver directly to your customers. You can do so via e-mail, direct mail pieces, telephone calls, and so on— anything that keeps you contacting your customers one-on-one over time.

By contacting and staying fresh with your customers, you will generate more repeat business. Use your ongoing communication efforts to tell customers about new products, services, and special deals you have for them to generate the most sales. Use any possible reason to contact them—a holiday, their birthday, your company's anniversary, and so on. Alternatively, you can contact them for no reason at all.

Keep in mind that not all of your communications should or must *sell* your customers something. You can—and should— communicate simply to further cement your brand in their heads and position yourself as the go-to company. If you're featured in the news, send them a clipping or an e-mail with a link. If you wrote an article that they may find helpful, send it to them. Stay fresh in any way you can and position your company as the authority and solver of their needs, and they will come back to you.

To ensure you implement or improve your ongoing customer communications, answer the following questions:

- How will you continuously communicate with your customers? What formats (e.g., e-mail, direct mail, telephone) will you use?
- On what occasions (e.g., company event, client's birthday) will you contact customers?
- What other kinds of quality content or information can you give customers besides updates about sales so that you aren't always pitching them?
- Who in your organization will you assign to manage ongoing customer communications?

In answering these questions, let me give you some examples of companies who have done it right:

- My business's accounting firm, which sends me a monthly newsletter in the mail with new tax information and tips. They aren't selling anything, but rather are providing a valuable service. I appreciate the newsletters, and they keep the accounting firm in the front of my mind. The result? I have continued to use this firm for years and have referred others to them.
- JetBlue Airways sends me a birthday e-mail every year. The company also e-mails me discounted flight opportunities several times each month.

- The US Lacrosse Association often e-mails me articles on how to be a better lacrosse dad and links to videos showing skills to teach my son and daughter.
- My friend Dustin Mathews is the cofounder of Speaking Empire, a great company that helps speakers achieve more success. After attending one of his events, I started receiving a monthly package in the mail from him which included a newsletter and an audio CD on which Dustin interviews an expert on a timely business topic. I also started getting letters from Dustin about his upcoming events.

In all of these cases, I buy more from these organizations because they continue to communicate with me, and I don't consider purchasing from their competition.

2. Loyalty Programs

In addition to ongoing communications, you can establish customer loyalty programs that encourage customers to keep coming back to you. Examples of loyalty programs include the following:

- Buy 10 (or another number) and get 1 free (coffee shops and barbers use this model quite often).
- Give customers reward dollars or points they can only redeem or accumulate when they make future purchases from you.
- Provide membership or discount cards. Give VIP cards (free or paid) or discount cards that give customers discounts on certain products or special access that non-card holders don't get.

To ensure you add loyalty programs to your business, answer the following questions:

- What type of loyalty program(s) might you be able to implement in your business?
- How will they work?
- Who in your organization will be in charge of developing and managing these program(s)?

Salsa Fresca Grill is a local burrito restaurant close to the gym I frequent after work each day. When you purchase 10 meals there, you get 1 free. Because of this, I pick up dinner for my family there approximately twice a month. Without it, I would be surprised if I went there twice per year.

3. Continuity or Membership Programs

Continuity or membership programs are a way to generate revenues from clients and keep them loyal. In addition to creating ongoing revenue, continuity programs dramatically increase your firm's overall value and make it more appealing to acquirers because you have a source of ongoing and residual revenues.

DVD-, book-, cigar-, and wine-of-the-month clubs are great examples of continuity programs that allow companies to sell their products to customers on an ongoing basis. Likewise, many service firms set up ongoing programs to service their clients every month, thus generating sales from their customers on an ongoing basis.

Here are some ideas for adding a continuity or membership program to your business:

- Subscriptions (magazines generally use the subscription model)
- Service contracts (I pay my oil provider for a service contract so it will repair my boiler should it break down)

- Licensing fees (many software companies offer a one-time product payment plus ongoing licensing fees to use the product and access upgrades)
- Recurring retainers (many firms such as PR agencies charge recurring monthly retainers)

It's important to note that the recurring or ongoing revenue method you use may be a *new* product or service you devise. For example, if you own a hardware store, you may not think getting recurring revenues is possible. But what if you charged ongoing (e.g., monthly, quarterly, or annual) fees for customers to:

- Get 15 percent discounts on all of your merchandise?
- Attend weekly or monthly demos you put together?
- Receive a newsletter or magazine showing how to build certain items?
- Do home walk-throughs to see if they need any repairs or hardware?

Take a moment to brainstorm ways in which you could add a continuity or membership program to your business.

BREAKING THE CAMEL'S BACK

This chapter and the last showed you a variety of ways to dramatically strengthen each of the four aspects of your marketing system. As I discussed previously, merely beating your competitors by 20 percent on each of these aspects can allow you to generate 2.3 times your competitor's profits.

Among other things, this will allow you to advertise in places in which they can't afford, further cementing your market dominance. Additionally, there are two further marketing tactics you should employ to ensure your success.

Referrals

The first of these is referrals, perhaps the most important and underutilized technique there is. Let's start with the math on referrals, and assume that your competitors get few to no referrals. You then establish a referral program that results in one new customer for every customer served. Doing so will immediately double your results. You will generate 4.6 times more profits than your competitors.

Yes—it's *that* powerful. Referrals are both a technique for maximizing customer value and for lead generation. The following are key to establishing a great referral program.

To begin, you need to *earn* referrals. You need to provide a valuable product or service that satisfies your customer. Once you do that, you simply need to ask for referrals, which, as you might imagine, companies rarely do. Consider the number of companies from whom *you* purchase each week. What percentage of them asks you to refer someone else? Generally, the answer is less than 1 percent.

You also can—but don't need to—offer incentives when asking for referrals. The incentive that the person they refer will be better off after using your product or service is generally enough.

Here are two examples of good referral systems at work. Earlier, I mentioned that Growthink uses a virtual receptionist company called Ruby Receptionists to answer incoming calls to our main telephone number. After using the service for seven months, I received an e-mail from Ruby with a referral request. Their offer: When you refer a new client and they sign up, Ruby will waive the client's setup fee and give you a $50 gift card. A second example is from the gym at which I've been a member for six years. Each year I get four e-mails from the gym with their "refer a friend and receive $100" offer.

It is critically important to ask for referrals often and to ask in the right way. With regards to the former, research shows that it generally takes five to seven impressions of a product until we make a buying decision. The same holds true with referrals. Sure, some people will give a referral the first time you ask them. But for most, it will take you asking a second, third, or even fourth or fifth time.

To ensure you're asking the right way, frame your referral request based on what you know about the customer. For example, "Who else do you know from your block that might need this product?" or "Who else on the planning committee of the National Marketing Association might benefit from this service?" By framing the referral request this way, you get customers to visualize the people they know and better identify those who could use your product or service.

Testing

Every marketing tactic I have shared with you in this chapter is proven either by one of my own businesses or by one of my clients.

However, the odds are that you will fail at some of these tactics. Why? Because you need to apply and test each tactic in your business to determine how to *best employ it.*

For example, let's consider the tactic of increasing your prices. If your current price is $35, should you try $42, $49, or $60? Which type of offer should you use to increase conversion rates? A guarantee offer? A premium offer? Both? Which products or services should you bundle together to create a package?

I don't know the answer, and although you might have a good idea as to what might work, the only people who know for sure are your customers. Whenever you launch changes, be sure to test them. Fortunately, you now know about KPIs and have a financial dashboard that you can use to record your results.

For example, test raising the price on one of your products or services on the first of next month. Let the test run until at least 100 customer see the new price. Then do the math. Did your profits go up? Did they go down? If they went up, then your higher price should become your new baseline price against you will conduct further tests. Yes, you should always be testing to further improve performance.

As marketing consultant Jay Abraham once said, "Your customers are geniuses, they know exactly what they want." For *you* to find out what your customers want, you need to test. Once you find the winners to your tests, you will dominate your market.

In this chapter and the last, you learned the best tactics and strategies to build a comprehensive marketing system that dramatically improves your marketing success. Work on improving each aspect of your system and you will dominate your market. In Chapter 10, you will document your chosen strategies into the marketing plan section of your business plan. Before we get to that, we need to ensure you have the right people working for you and the correct management structure in place. We will cover this in the next chapter.

CHAPTER 9

DEVELOPING YOUR HR PLAN

You learned in Chapter 6 about systematizing your business—specifically, how developing systems and processes creates massive value for your company. Hopefully, you recall one of the key points of that chapter: You want your business to be *process*-dependent rather than *people*-dependent. In other words, the ideal company has such good systems and processes in place that virtually any new employee could come in and perform with competence.

I'm sure you can imagine how valuable such a situation would be to your company, as well as to acquirers, who could easily add your turnkey operation to their business.

However, even if you have great processes, you'll want great employees, too; those who will have the skill sets needed to perform the processes you've put in place. For example, even if you have a detailed process for rebooting a server, a computer-illiterate employee probably couldn't do it. On the other hand, if you hired an employee with computer and technical skills, you could feel confident that they could execute on that process, improve the process over time, and complete the process even if unforeseen or catastrophic circumstances arose.

Great employees help you build better systems and improve them over time. They will also help develop a great company culture that brings out the best in everyone.

IDENTIFYING ROLES AND NEEDS WITH ORGANIZATIONAL CHARTS

An organizational chart, or org chart, is a diagram the details the key roles in your company and the interrelations between these roles and the reporting structure. Typically, the diagram includes the head of the company (president or CEO) in a box at the top, and then boxes beneath that for each key role. Within these boxes are the names of both the role and the person who has been tasked with fulfilling that role.

Your org chart should include all your business' key functions (i.e., marketing, finance, operations, etc.) and you should drill down further as appropriate. For instance, within your marketing department you might include functions such as customer service, public relations, advertising and promotions, website development, and so on. Within your finance department, you might include accounting, bookkeeping, accounts payable, and customer billing.

The following is a sample org chart.

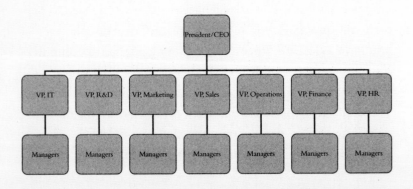

Unfortunately, most entrepreneurs and small business owners operate without an org chart. This is a big mistake. An org chart allows you to better manage your organization and determine what key roles you need to fill. Right now, as most small businesses do, you probably have employees occupying several positions on the org chart (and you yourself probably do many jobs). This is fine *for now*, but you need to start thinking bigger and about your end game, and to identify the roles you will need to fill as you grow. To achieve your vision, you must create three org charts: Your endgame org chart, your current org chart, and your annual org chart. Each of these are explained in more detail in the following sections.

YOUR ENDGAME ORG CHART

This book is called *Start at the End* for a reason. Strategizing in reverse should apply to all aspects of a business. This includes your human resource strategy, which is why the first org chart you need to create is your endgame org chart. If you don't know how you'd like your organization to look when fully built, you'll have no chance of creating it.

Your endgame org chart is the org chart you envision for your company when you reach your endgame—specifically, how your org chart will look once you have fully built the company you've envisioned. Think about the following questions when developing this:

- What company divisions or key functions will you have?
- Who will be running these divisions? What are the characteristics of these employees; for example, what will the resume include for the person who eventually runs your marketing department?

- What role will you perform?
- For how many people will you be directly responsible?
- What functions will stay within your organization rather than being outsourced to other organizations?

Your endgame org chart is not going to be 100 percent accurate. It will, however, get you thinking about the types of people you will need to hire and structures you'll have to put in place as you grow your company. As you build your annual org chart, you will ensure that you're progressing toward your desired endgame.

To help you understand how your org chart might need to look upon reaching your exit, look at the org charts of already successful companies. For example, if you are a manufacturing company, search online for the org charts of publicly traded manufacturing companies. From those, you can get a sense of the type of organization you will need to build. If you can't find such org charts for your industry, find the annual reports of publicly traded companies. In those reports, there is typically a section listing executive officers. Record the titles of these officers to understand the key functional categories you will need to develop.

YOUR CURRENT ORG CHART

Your current org chart is your org chart as it actually appears today. To create this, simply fill in your endgame org chart specifying who, if anyone, is currently performing the roles.

Keep in mind that you must include all roles in the chart, even those you are personally performing. For example, perhaps today you are the president of your company and manager of finances. If so, your org chart should list yourself as the president and as the VP of finance reporting to the president. Although it might seem odd to show you reporting to yourself, this structure will alert you to the need to eventually fill this position with someone with the appropriate skill set who can focus on it full time.

Give some serious thought to all the roles that you and your employees currently perform when building your current org chart. It's very likely that your name and the names of certain employees will appear multiple times on the chart. This signals that you might want to hire new employees to take over some of those positions.

Finally, include a box for all roles you are outsourcing—for example, IT or bookkeeping—on your org chart. In these boxes, list the name of the function and the outsourced firm or person who currently performs it.

For example, your current org chart may look like this:

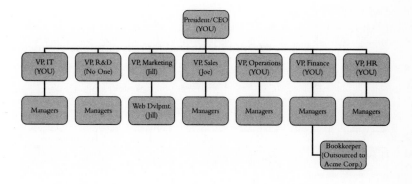

YOUR ANNUAL ORG CHART AND DETERMINING YOUR NEW HIRES THIS YEAR

The final org chart you need to create is your annual, or one-year, org chart. This will represent how you would like your company to look at the end of the coming year.

To create your annual org chart, start by looking at the boxes in your current org chart that are empty or that have a name that also appears in another role in the chart. These are the functions that you need to consider filling this year.

In addition, to identify additional new roles to fill and prioritize the order in which you need to fill roles, consider the annual plans that you've been developing while reading this book. Which new opportunities have you decided to pursue? What financial metrics have you set? What business assets must you build? What systems do you need to establish? What new marketing channels will you pursue?

Assess which hires are critical to achieving these goals and prioritize them. For example, if you determined you were going to pursue PR this year, hiring a full-time or outsourced PR person could be a key hire, as suggested in the sample annual org chart:

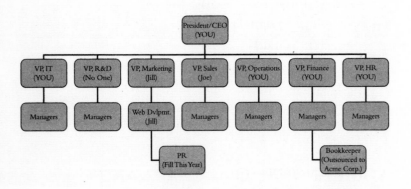

Be sure to develop a comprehensive job description specifying the requirements of the job and the skill sets needed by an employee to expertly complete each of the new roles you identify.

One final thing to consider when creating your annual org chart and determining your hiring needs is that it is virtually impossible for you to expertly manage more than seven direct reports that perform disparate tasks. Why? To get the most value out of these employees, you should be meeting with and coaching them for at least 30 minutes per month. That many direct reports takes too many hours to manage.

If you are currently managing more than seven employees, you need to hire additional managers in your organization. Then you (and they) will have fewer people to manage and can manage each more effectively.

Whether you have high-growth aspirations such as Facebook or Google, or you wish to steadily grow into a highly successful business in your market, creating your three org charts is essential. I have seen when working with my clients that there is great satisfaction each year as you grow. You start with a relatively bare org chart and start completing it with hires, and by year's end, you have the org chart you envisioned for that year. And that org chart starts looking more and more like the end-game org chart you developed.

Go to www.startatend.com to download worksheets to help you complete your org charts.

HIRING NEW EMPLOYEES

You now know, thanks to your org chart, what key hires your company needs to make. Even if you have the best systems and processes in the world, your company's performance will suffer if you don't have quality employees implementing them.

In fact, as renowned *Good to Great* author Jim Collins states, "The most important decisions that business people make are not *what* decisions but *who* decisions" (with "who" referring to the employees in your organization). As such, this section will teach you several strategies for more effectively hiring new employees.

Of biggest concern is management guru Peter Drucker's estimation that the average manager makes hiring mistakes 50 percent of the time. Clearly, that's far too many hiring mistakes. To make matters worse, according to Dr. Jeff Smart—bestselling author of *Who*, a book that focuses on how to hire correctly— a bad hiring decision costs the business 15 times the faulty hire's salary.

This is precisely why making good hiring decisions are absolutely critical to your company's success.

The best way I have found to judge the potential success of a new hire is to watch what I call *real game plays*—a concept best illustrated with the story of San Francisco 49ers head scout Tony Razzano. Early in his career, Razzano made a big mistake. He watched a young punter named Jim Miller punting the ball in an empty stadium, and Miller was absolutely phenomenal. He was punting the ball amazing distances. As a result, Razzano suggested the team draft Jim Miller.

Unfortunately, when it came to real game plays, Miller *wasn't* a great punter. It's very different when somebody is punting in an empty stadium from when he is being chased down by large men who really want the football. This is similar to a job candidate who seems perfect during their interview but who fails to perform well when actually on the job.

Tony Razzano used this experience to change his recruiting strategy, ensuring he always watched at least 200 actual game plays for each player he recommended. This new strategy allowed Razzano to find and draft legendary quarterback Joe Montana as the 82nd pick in the 1979 NFL draft and wide receiver Jerry Rice as the 10th player in the 1985 draft.

By comprehensively assessing these players' skills in real world situations—or in real game plays—Razzano was able to spot talent that many others couldn't see.

So how do you assess prospective employees on real game plays, particularly when you don't have their past performances on video like Tony Razzano did?

There are two ways. You can evaluate their current real game plays by giving them tests to see how they might perform in the role you have open. You can also judge their past real game plays by asking them about their performance in past jobs and calling references to confirm the validity of their responses.

Regarding current real game plays, you'll want to devise tests for prospective employees. For example, give the prospect a writing assignment if you have an open position that requires writing or a research project for an open research position. If the prospect does a mediocre job on either assignment, they're not going to magically start a doing better job when you hire them. Treat the assignment as their best possible work without the training you're going to give them if they're hired.

Coming up with real game play ideas that judge a prospect's performance is harder for some roles than it is for other. You can get creative, however. For example, let's say that your company sells a technical product. In this case, it can be hard to test a prospective salesperson's ability to sell it without technical training.

But you could tell the prospect that you doubt their ability to learn the technical aspects of the product to make enough sales. Good salespeople would combat your remark with a quality sales pitch on why they can learn the product's technical aspects and why you should hire them. A weak salesperson, however, would take the criticism and walk away. You want to hire the former.

You can also devise simple tasks for any prospective employees to perform and then assess them. How quickly did they perform? How accurate were they? Did they follow directions? You can learn quite a bit about prospective hires from even simple tests. Because these tests can more accurately predict future performance than all the interview questions in the world, take the time to conduct them.

Now that you know how to assess a prospective hire's real game plays, you need to know how to get good prospects to assess. You can take the steps in the following section to achieve that:

1. Document the Job Responsibilities, Position Criteria, and Success Metrics of the Position You Need Filled

Specifically, cite the job responsibilities or role to be performed (e.g., sell our products to new customers) and the required position criteria (e.g., five years of sales experience, proficiency in using CRM systems). It's also crucial to document what success looks like (e.g., a good hire will be able to generate $50K in sales per month within 4 months and $100K in sales per month within 1 year). Without these established success metrics, neither you nor the employee will understand what's expected.

2. Source New Employees

The best way for sourcing new employees is via referrals. You can get referrals in a variety of ways: from employees (the best source), your advisors, friends, colleagues, and other contacts. Don't hesitate to ask around and see who people know who could be great for an open position. Offer your current employees a reward for new hires they refer that work out (to be paid 90 days after their referral is hired and has thus proven themselves).

Other potential sources for finding new employees include hiring professional recruiters or firms, posting on job boards, getting ads in trade journals, and buying classified ads on sites such as Craigslist. If you are trying to fill a critical role in your company, consider making more of an investment in finding this person, because the right person will yield considerably better results than the wrong one. For example, in its early years, eBay paid executive recruiting firm Kindred Partners to find and hire Meg Whitman. Whitman turned eBay into a multibillion-dollar company.

3. Interview the Candidates

As discussed previously, the most accurate way to predict an employee's potential success is to view their current and past real game plays, both by conducting tests to see how they might perform in the role you have available and by asking questions to learn how they performed in the roles listed on their resumes. Pose specific questions about how they performed, how performance was at the company before they started the job versus once they were engaged, and how past bosses would rate their performance.

You want to have multiple people within your organization interview prospective hires. This ensures that you've thoroughly vetted prospects for both job competence and fit within the company's culture.

4. Check References

Another critical step is to contact potential employees' prior employers to ensure their claims of success in past game plays are true. Confirm the prospects' stated claims and ask probing questions about their greatest strengths and weaknesses to gain more information with which to make your decision.

Following these steps will ensure you will build a team of high quality employees—as long as you don't cut corners. Although it's tempting to take some shortcuts to hire more quickly, doing so will leave you with a team of mediocre players. This will force you to work twice as hard and may keep you from achieving the growth you desire.

GETTING THE MOST OUT OF YOUR EMPLOYEES

Even if you have enough employees and you've hired the *right* employees, you still have a lot of work to do to get the most out of the people who work for you.

In fact, most businesses fail in this regard. According to *Fortune Magazine*, only 14 percent of CEOs indicated that their organizations did an effective job of implementing the strategies set in their strategic plans. Additionally, the Balanced Scorecard Collaborative found that "90 percent of organizations fail to execute their strategic plans successfully." Perhaps, most important, the Balanced Scorecard Collaborative also found that 95 percent of a typical workforce doesn't understand its organization's strategy.

Consider that for a moment: *95 percent* of your employees do not understand your organization's strategy. How can they possibly perform at their peak if this is so? How could they possibly make the right decisions when conducting their jobs?

Therefore, the first thing you need to do to get the most out of your employees is to show them your strategic plan. In fact, you want to involve your managers and top employees in its creation. Get their input about your organization's strengths, and have them brainstorm and assess new growth strategies with you.

Whether your employees are involved in developing or simply viewing your business's strategic plan, they must clearly understand it. If they don't understand where the organization is heading, they can't do their jobs effectively. This goes back to what we discussed at the beginning of this book: That every player on the New York Giants knows the goal of their organization (to reach and win the Super Bowl).

Of course, this thinking doesn't give the New York Giants a competitive advantage because every other football team also operates with this focus and understanding. Getting *your* employees to understand and buy into the vision and plan, however, will give you a sizable advantage because the vast majority of businesses don't do this. Studies show that most businesses have dissatisfied employees comprising the majority of their workforce. We see this daily when we encounter disenfranchised workers at businesses we call or frequent. Conversely, when employees know the company's vision and plan, they will be happier, more motivated, and able to make decisions that support the company's goals in their day-to-day work.

Another way to get the most value from your employees is to have them document their job responsibilities. Although this may seem boring and unimportant, you will realize substantial improvements in employee productivity if you do this exercise in the following way.

To begin, write out the job responsibilities of all new hires—something most business owners must do when creating job ads for openings. However, most business owners neglect a very important fact: Jobs change over time. Consider an employee you hired two years ago. Were they doing exactly what was included in the list of job responsibilities a month after they were hired? Were they doing at least one thing new or different? How about 6 months into the job? A year? Two years? How many responsibilities had evolved over that period of time?

As you're probably recognizing, job descriptions inevitably change as your company grows. This is why it's important that your employees understand their responsibilities to best complete them, and that *you* understand them to best manage them.

I recommend you do the following exercise with your employees each year in order to accomplish this.

> Have each of your employees write up a job description of their current role.

You'll learn an important lesson by doing this: What *you* think they are doing and what *they* think they are doing are often very different.

The second part of this exercise is to ask employees how they think their job performance should be judged. I phrased this question as follows in my organization:

> How do you think your performance should be judged? For example, if you were to be given solely a variable salary (don't worry, this isn't going to happen), how would we determine whether your performance warrants a lot versus a little pay?

Once again, there will generally be a considerable disconnect between what you (the business owner and manager) think and what employees think. The good news is that closing this gap ensures that each of your employees is fully aware of their responsibilities and what constitutes optimal performance. Without this, employees will be clueless and unmotivated.

In this chapter, you identified the human resources you will need to reach your end game. You created your endgame org chart, your current org chart, and the annual org chart, which you need to achieve by the end of this year to progress toward your vision. You also learned best practices for recruiting quality employees to your company and keeping them motivated. At this point, you have fully developed each of the key aspects (e.g., marketing plan, human resources plan, etc.) of your strategic or business plan. In the next chapter, you will learn how to document your strategic plan. By getting your plan on paper, it will better serve as a road map to guide you and your team toward completing your annual and long-term goals.

CHAPTER 10

DOCUMENTING YOUR STRATEGIC PLAN

In the preceding chapters, you learned what to do to build a thriving business.

You identified where you want to go and the phases involved in getting there. I guided you in recognizing which opportunities will foster your growth. You identified which business assets to build and which financial metrics to track to ensure your success. You learned how to systematize your business so it can run without you. And you determined which marketing tactics would allow you to best maximize profits.

Having done all that, you should feel pretty good right now. But there is one critical step left: Documenting your strategy into a strategic plan.

As specified previously, a strategic plan is a detailed road map for achieving your goals. Your success will skyrocket when you document your road map on paper because:

- The process of documenting your plan and then reading it gets your subconscious used to the fact that you *can* accomplish it
- A documented plan eliminates confusion over what needs to be done

- The plan will show your employees what needs to be accomplished and by when, encouraging all employees to work together in achieving your goals
- The plan can get other readers, perhaps board members, advisors, investors, potential management hires, and consultants, up to speed on your business quickly and allow them to give valuable advice

Although your strategic plan should include your long-term vision, you'll lay out the actual plan for a period of one year. Trying to plan beyond a year is fruitless because many things in your business and market will inevitably change. You'll need to adjust your plan as these changes occur. No matter what happens, however, your plan will always propel you toward your long-term vision. This means that even if markets change, your company will be getting closer to achieving the long term success you envision as you follow your plan.

For example, a client of mine, Dakim, creates products to help prevent memory loss in seniors. The company's original product was a hardware and software solution that included a touch screen monitor for easy use by seniors. However, as more and more nursing homes and households with seniors installed computers, the dual hardware and software solution became obsolete. However, because the company had continued to develop assets (e.g., installs in nursing homes, brand awareness, improvements to software), it was able to seamlessly transition to a software only solution and continue its growth.

THE 10 SECTIONS OF A STRATEGIC PLAN

The benefits of having your strategic plan on paper, as discussed previously, far outweigh the cost of the time needed to prepare the document. In fact, your strategic plan should be 20 pages or less—strive for brevity.

Your strategic plan will include 10 sections. If you have developed a business plan before, when you read each of the sections, you will probably identify several differences between my strategic plan and that of a traditional business plan.

This difference comes from the different meanings of the terms business plan and strategic plan. Although the terms are often used synonymously, I am distinguishing the phrases based on their use. Specifically, business plans are typically prepared and used by companies who are seeking funding, whereas strategic plans are prepared by companies seeking growth.

Although many companies want to achieve both, business plans prepared for funding need to accomplish certain goals that strategic plans do not. Specifically, business plans need to educate the prospective investor or lender. You must explain the size and nature of your market. You must identify the main competitors and explain your competitive differentiation. You must also specify the customers you are targeting and the details of each customer segment.

Conversely, although your strategic plan uses this same information, there is no need to explicitly document it because it is not actionable. For example, stating that the size of your market is $300 million isn't something you can act on. Your strategic plan lays out your strategy and the actions your company will take to execute on that strategy. It lays out the precise goals and milestones you need to achieve.

Specifically, you will see that traditional business planning sections such as your company analysis (which details the history and background of your company), market/industry analysis, competitive analysis, and customer analysis sections will be omitted. Certain sections have been added, such as company vision statements, opportunities to pursue, goals and milestones, financial metrics and KPIs, business assets, and your systematization plan.

While reading this section, I encourage you to think about and write your strategic plan. When you finish this book, your plan will be complete, and you will be ready to dramatically grow your business.

Executive Summary

This first section of your strategic plan should summarize the key points of each of the other sections in about one to three pages.

In writing hundreds of strategic plans, I discovered I like to complete the executive summary section last. It is easiest to do it this way: You simply include the most important points from each of the other sections. Because of its short size, the executive summary will clearly not give all the details of your plan. However, it should give enough information to give readers a solid understanding of the company's vision and key goals, and it should be exciting enough to make them to want to read more.

The ideal length of the full strategic plan is between 10 and 15 pages. This gives you enough space to provide the level of detail you need while keeping the reader engaged; if it's too long, people won't want to invest the time to read it.

Company Vision Statements

As discussed in Chapter 1, in this section you will enter your customer- and business-focused visions, including your desired endgame, the financial metrics you want to achieve, and business assets you plan to build by the time you exit your business.

Opportunities to Pursue

The next section of your plan will document the opportunities you have chosen to pursue. It's not only important to write down what opportunities your company is planning to go after but to answer why as well. This will help readers see the opportunities stacked up against:

- Your company's strengths
- The Ansoff matrix/product/market expansion grid as discussed in Chapter 2
- Market criteria (market size and trends, competitive gaps, etc.)
- Your financial projections

These details will help readers (such as employees) better understand the strategic importance of pursuing these new opportunities, which will improve their buy-in.

Goals and Milestones

In this section of your plan, you will document your exit or five-year, one-year, quarterly, and monthly financial metric and business asset goals.

You will include the goals and milestones you developed in Chapters 3, 4, and 5 after you identified the financial metric and business asset goals you hope to achieve in these time periods. In your plan, start by presenting your goals for the longest time period (e.g., your exit or five-year goals) and then present the shorter time periods—your annual, and then quarterly and monthly goals.

A lot of description is not required. Instead, simply list the time period followed by bullet points listing your goals for each time period.

Financial Metrics and KPIs

This section will document the KPIs you will track in your business, such as sales, number of new customers, customer satisfaction, and customer conversion rates.

In subsequent versions of your plan, you will show which KPIs you have historically tracked and what your goals are for each for the upcoming period. You will also add new KPIs to track going forward.

Business Assets

In this section you will document the business assets you need to develop in the coming year, and more important, the individual projects you must complete to build them. Include your Gantt charts, as discussed in Chapter 5, showing each project's projected start and end dates, project manager assignments, and how the projects interrelate as applicable.

Systematization Plan

Your systematization plan should detail the new systems you have prioritized for creation, including each system's name and goal, as well as who will lead the development of building it.

Marketing Plan

This section of your strategic plan will detail your marketing plan. You should start by documenting your customer needs; you can do this by including answers to the key questions you documented in Chapter 7, such as what their demographic and psychographic profiles are and what needs, wants, or desires your product or service fulfills.

You should then provide your strategies for improving each of the four aspects of your marketing system as you learned in Chapters 7 and 8.

To improve *lead generation*, specify what new lead generation sources you will try in the coming year, such as direct mail, radio advertising, and PR.

To improve *conversion rates*, document your current USP and ways you could strengthen it. Discuss how you will improve your offers and sales scripts. Cite ways you will increase your social proof. Include details on how you can better nurture your leads and improve prospective customers' perceptions of your company.

To optimize *transaction prices*, detail your strategies for raising prices, offering product or service packages, upselling and cross-selling, or increasing order sizes.

To *maximize lifetime customer value*, document how you will leverage ongoing communications, loyalty programs, continuity or membership programs, or referral programs.

Human Resources Plan

The human resources section of your strategic plan ensures that you have the right people to execute on the opportunities you've identified.

The first part of this section should show the three organization charts you developed in Chapter 9. As you recall, these charts include your endgame, current, and annual org charts that identify all the key roles in your company and the interrelations between them.

Beneath the annual org chart, list your current employees (including yourself) and detail their key roles and responsibilities. Finally, identify new employees that you *need to hire this year.* These individuals will fill missing roles in the annual org chart or roles that you are performing and must assign to other people.

For each of the new hires you need, list the job title, key responsibilities, key requirements of the ideal applicant, and the date you expect the hire to join your company.

Financial Projections

This section includes your strategic plan's financial implications: Specifically, the financial projections you created when determining the opportunities to pursue. You want to break out these financial projections by month so you can judge your actual performance based on the plan.

Be sure to consider increased costs from new hires, product development, and so on in your projections, as well as cost savings from systematization.

Note that within the body of your strategic plan, only include the topline financial projections. These are the big financial line items such as revenues, cost of goods sold, and salary expenses. Conversely, detailed financial information, such as salary expenses broken down by each employee, can be included as an appendix to the plan as applicable.

Go to www.startatend.com to download a checklist for writing your strategic plan.

KEEPING YOUR PLAN CURRENT

Once you have completed your first strategic plan, you should review it every month and use it to establish a formal monthly planning meeting. You and each of your key managers should attend the meeting.

This meeting is the time to judge your financial performance and business assets you've built against your plans. Ideally, you performed according to plan. If you didn't, you need to determine why and adjust your strategy and goals for the next month.

Specifically, I suggest scheduling the following 13 strategic plan meetings to keep your strategic plan current and to ensure you are achieving your stated goals and progressing toward your endgame. Each time you set the next quarter's or month's goals, be sure to update the goals and milestones section of your strategic plan to reflect the new goals. (These meeting dates assume you operate on a calendar year.)

1. Middle to end of December: Review current year and current quarter's results, set annual and first quarter goals for the following year, and create annual business plan

2. Beginning of January: Review December results, set January goals

3. Beginning of February: Review January results, set February goals

4. Beginning of March: Review February results, set March goals

5. Beginning of April: Review March and first quarter results, set April and second quarter goals

6. Beginning of May: Review April results, set May goals

7. Beginning of June: Review May results, set June goals

8. Beginning of July: Review June and second quarter results, set July and third quarter goals

9. Beginning of August: Review July results, set August goals

10. Beginning of September: Review August results, set September goals

11. Beginning of October: Review September and third quarter results, set October and fourth quarter goals

12. Beginning of November: Review October results, set November goals
13. Beginning of December: Review November results, set December goals

As you hold these monthly meetings and review your strategic plan and results, here are some examples of what you may encounter:

- *Projects not completed on time.* Particularly as you first adapt the tactics described herein, such as establishing a series of projects to be completed each month, you will notice projects that remain unfinished at the end of the month. Because most businesses are unaccustomed to working in such a focused manner, you and your team may have trouble estimating how long projects take to complete at first. When a project remains undone at the end of a month or quarter, you should assess what went wrong and identify corrective actions. You will need to modify your Gantt charts to push back the date on other projects so you can complete the outstanding ones.

- *New business assets or strategies not working.* Let's say, for example, that in January you decided to test direct mail as a new marketing channel. You succeeded in completing your January project of mailing out 1,000 pieces of mail. However, near the end of February, you tallied the results of your direct mail campaign and found it to be ineffective. At this point, you must determine whether you will try to improve your direct mail marketing or start your next marketing channel, perhaps radio advertising, which you had slated to begin in March. Unless your direct mail campaign absolutely bombed, I suggest spending the next month or two trying to improve direct mail to make it work and pushing radio advertising back two months. Once again, as you get used to operating in such a structured manner with defined monthly goals, you will begin to do a better job with setting goals and giving yourself more time to develop new projects and test new marketing channels.

- *New ideas have arisen.* When you assess your actual KPIs against projected KPIs, you will be satisfied with some results and disappointed with others. For example, you may find that customer satisfaction went up, but your conversion rate on new customers went down. In this case, you should brainstorm new ideas to boost conversion rates. Hopefully you'll come up with a new idea, such as sending your prospective clients a gift in the mail. Once again, executing on this new idea will require you to push other planned projects back further. This is okay; it's a judgment call you need to make about which projects are a priority. This is why you have these pre-established 13 meetings each year. Rather than making these prioritization decisions on a whim, you will discuss them in these meetings, giving you and your managers the time and data at your disposal to make the best possible decisions.

- *New opportunities have arisen.* Each week, you will be alerted to new potential growth opportunities. A potential partner may contact you, or you may learn about a new technology or social network your business may want to adapt. In some cases, these opportunities are merely shiny objects, as discussed in Chapter 3. In other cases, these are legitimate opportunities you should pursue. As suggested in Chapter 3, when you come across these opportunities, you should not act on them immediately, but rather save them for review during your next planning meeting. At these meetings, discuss these new opportunities and whether they merit pursuing. If they do, add them to your list of projects to be completed in the next month or quarter, once again pushing back other projects you want completed.

During your monthly planning sessions, you will see the progress your company is making. You should also see the positive effects on your profit and loss statement as you methodically execute on your business. On the other hand, you might initially be a little disappointed by the amount of projects that you still must complete. Please remain positive: Remember that as you grow, you will be adding systems and personnel that allow you to complete more projects more quickly over time. You will eventually reach and complete each of the key projects as you grow your business and close in on your end goal.

In this chapter, you learned how to compile all the strategizing and goal-setting you completed in previous chapters into a comprehensive yet concise strategic plan you and your team can follow to achieve your short-term and long-term goals. You also learned how to establish monthly planning meetings and how to use them to assess and revise your goals. This will allow you to remain nimble yet focused on your goals.

In the next chapter, I discuss productivity techniques that allow you and your company to progress and more quickly reach your goals.

CHAPTER 11

HOW TO PROGRESS
EVEN FASTER

We've discussed previously how the business owner—you—are the bottleneck in most companies. If you were able to clone yourself, you would be able to more quickly execute on your business plan and your business would grow much faster and more successfully. Because cloning yourself is not a viable option, the next best thing is to dramatically boost your productivity, which will have the same effect.

For example, consider the productivity challenge faced by NASA back in 1970. A fault in the electrical system of the *Apollo 13* spaceship produced an explosion that caused a loss of electrical power and failure of both oxygen tanks. Getting the astronauts home safely required new software to be written immediately. But there was a problem: such software would normally have taken three months to create. Through effective planning and productivity tactics, however, NASA created the software in just three days and brought the pilots home safely.

NASA realized an increase in productivity times 30. At such a pace, they could have accomplished three years of work in one month. In one year, they could have accomplished 30 years of work. Imagine what that would mean to your company if

3 years of work in one month

you could accomplish in one month what your competition would require three years to do. Although creating a sustainable increase in productivity that great is impossible, doubling your productivity isn't, and it will give you a sizable competitive advantage and allow you to realize your goals faster.

Most business owners falsely assume they are working at "peak productivity" simply because they are working hard or long hours. Yet most are severely lacking. The good news is that making a few simple changes will allow you to easily boost performance, which in turn will help you better execute on your business plan and improve results.

Read on to see how. Some of the ideas in the following sections relate to personal productivity and some to the productivity of your organization. Once you employ the personal productivity tactics yourself and see the benefits, teach them to your employees to reap the full benefits.

How to Identify and Build Projects into Your Schedule

Throughout this book, you have undoubtedly identified numerous projects you'd like to accomplish, from creating new products to building new systems to developing scripts to increase your sales conversions. However, going from "it would be great to accomplish these ten things" to actually completing them is often very challenging. It's where most business owners break down. Specifically, most business owners can't find the time to complete these projects, and thus their great ideas and plans don't get done. As a result, they don't build the businesses they envisioned.

The following five steps will help you identify your highest priority projects and tasks and show you how to methodically complete them in less time. This way, you can complete your projects and build the company of your dreams.

Step 1 →   *Master List*

Create Your Overall To-Do List

In your strategic plan, you documented several projects and tasks that your organization needs to accomplish, including several that you need to spearhead. The first thing you need to do to boost your productivity and accomplish the goals you laid out is to clearly list of all the specific tasks that you, as business owner, need to complete. To do so, you should create and maintain an Overall To-Do List that includes *all* of these tasks.

The process of documenting these items purges your brain of all the tasks that are nagging you. Writing down the most critical assignments will allow you to concentrate better on them. It also reduces your stress and clears your mind, thereby making you much more creative and effective.

For example, how many times have you been concentrating on completing a task, such as writing a report or analyzing a statement, when some kind of to-do thought such as "oh, I really need to e-mail Joe Smith" popped into your mind? It's no secret that these distractions effectively ruin your concentration and diminish your productivity.

These mental interruptions occur much less frequently when you maintain and constantly add to your Overall To-Do List, which allows you to get much more work accomplished.

However, it's equally important to ensure you don't become overwhelmed by a large Overall To-Do List. In most cases, you will *never* complete everything on it. As you constantly prioritize it, certain items will keep getting pushed down. This is ok because these are generally items that you shouldn't be doing anyway.

Although I skim my Overall To-Do List every month to determine my priorities (learn more about this in the following section), I only do a thorough review of the entire list once per year. When I do, I see tons of items at the bottom that have been sitting there for months. In virtually all these cases, I simply delete the items. I had clearly been able to grow my business without completing them, so I'm glad I didn't waste time on them.

Step 2 →   *Quad II Business Buildy*
                                              Tasks

Prioritize Your List

Your next step is to constantly prioritize your Overall To-Do List, and the best model for understanding how to prioritize is to use the following four quadrants framework:

	Urgent	Not Urgent
Important *delegate* →	- Customer crises - Upset employees - Deadlines to create or reply to a proposal	- Marketing strategies - Product development - Creating new systems
Not Important	- Phone call from someone trying to sell you a new service - Got a minute requests - Most e-mail requests	- Coffee breaks - Reading the newspaper - Watching a funny video online

In the top left quadrant are the important and urgent items. These are typically the daily fire-fighting exercises that most business owners and employees take care of, such as the upset client call. It's urgent, it's important, and you need to deal with it as soon as it occurs. Therefore people spend a great deal of their time on these important and urgent issues.

The top right quadrant is important but *not* urgent, which should also be your priority, but is unfortunately the area most business owners leave undone. This includes tasks such as executing on your annual plan, conducting employee performance reviews, and developing new products. I commend you right now that you are doing something (i.e., reading this book) that is important to you—and yet *not* urgent—that is going to massively improve your success and the success of your company.

The bottom left quadrant is not important, yet urgent items—things that are not important but are right in your face. This is a telephone call from a prospective vendor, or your coworker or employee saying, "Hey, do you have a minute? I need a hand with something," or perhaps answering a unique question posed by a customer. These items are not really important because they don't get you closer to achieving your goals.

Finally, the bottom right quadrant is not important and not urgent—taking a coffee break, reading the paper, or getting lunch with a colleague.

The key point of the four quadrants is that you absolutely need to prioritize quadrant number two (top right quadrant)—the important and *not* urgent tasks. These are the tasks that allow you to grow your business. Although it can be difficult for a lot of business owners, you must start judging all of the items in your Overall To-Do List and prioritizing these important tasks because these are the ones that move you closer to achieving your goals.

Although someone needs to complete the quadrant one tasks, those that are both important and urgent (such as a customer crises), ideally that person should not be you. Rather, as much as possible, build systems to avoid having to complete these tasks in the first place. Delegate completion of the tasks to others. This leaves you more time to complete the critical quadrant two business-building tasks.

An Overall To Do LIST

Step 3

Break Down Your Priorities into Smaller Tasks

Mark Twain said: "The secret of getting ahead is getting started." Therefore, once you have identified your top priorities, you must get started by breaking your complex, overwhelming tasks into small, manageable tasks that can be completed more quickly. Then you can begin working on the first one.

Obviously, no individual task should take more than 8 hours if you're working approximately an 8-hour day. You're going to face interruptions every day unless you are working offsite. You therefore need to separate your tasks into *assignments that you can complete in two hours or less.*

2 hr or <

For example, let's say you want to write a report. You could break it down into the following two-hour subtasks:

- Do research
- Create the draft table of contents
- Outline Chapter 1
- Write Chapter 1
- Proof Chapter 1
- And so on

Step 4

Create Weekly and Daily To-Do Lists

You should create a list for yourself at the beginning of each week that details which key tasks and priorities you want to accomplish during the week. Keeping that list nearby and checking off items as you complete them is key to your success.

Likewise, you need to identify the to-dos from your weekly list that you need to accomplish each day. You can then see what you accomplished each day and create your to-do list for the next day. Do the same for your weekly list at the end of each week.

Review

Schedule Every Minute of Every Day

This is perhaps that most important piece of achieving your goals: To find a way to schedule every minute of every day. I know this might sound like a daunting task, but let me explain.

Parkinson's Law, first introduced by British historian Cyril Northcote Parkinson in a 1955 essay in *The Economist*, states that work expands to fill the time allotted to performing it. This means that if you designate three hours to complete a task, it's most likely going to take you the full three hours to get it done.

Most people go through their day without a minute by minute, hour by hour schedule. They do not have these deadlines and so they take longer to finish their tasks. So if, according to Parkinson's Law, you allocate three hours to working on a report—and spend that exact amount of time on it—you'll always stress and procrastinate and really work hard the last 15 minutes to accomplish the goal within the 3-hour period.

Now, let's say that you had only given yourself an hour to complete the report. You're going to work harder during that hour and be much more focused. You will complete virtually the same work—or even *better* work—in that hour.

Setting deadlines for tasks prompts you to complete them faster. You are much more focused on what you're doing, racing against the clock, but not in a bad way. This doesn't mean that you're creating stress. You're just engaging in a little friendly competition against the clock. You say to yourself, "It is 3:19; I have to complete this project by 4 o'clock because I have to get to the next meeting by then." That's when you start thinking, "Ok—so what exactly do I have to do to get this done?" Your mind starts working, you accomplish your tasks faster, and it's fun, because you're much more successful in a shorter period of time.

friendly competi-
against the clock

Most people cannot get work done at work because they are constantly getting pulled into meetings and conversations starting with "Do you have a minute to discuss this and that," or "please respond to this e-mail right away." Fortunately, there is a solution to this madness: Have a set calendar, and schedule *every minute of every day*.

A set calendar allows you to focus completely on one task at a time, allowing you to finish it faster and do a better job. Numerous studies have shown that multitasking actually *reduces productivity and performance*.

Schedule all of your priorities that you have reduced to smaller, two-hour projects. These go on your calendar first, and you can't let anything interfere with them. This way, interruptions can only occur during set times. If someone has a got a minute request or a customer has an urgent issue, they will simply have to wait until you're free (of course, you must also schedule free time on your calendar to handle these issues). Essentially, you are creating meetings with yourself on your calendar, which is what the most successful entrepreneurs in the world do.

My own specific strategy for achieving my goals is as follows: On Monday morning each week, I review my Overall To-Do List and my monthly goals and decide what I must accomplish during that coming week. I then divide those tasks into smaller tasks that never take more than two hours each to complete.

I then schedule my entire week's calendar with those smaller tasks. During those calendared times, I am unreachable. I will not answer the phone or e-mail or allow myself to be interrupted with questions. I *do* schedule times on my calendar to answer e-mails, return phone calls, handle questions, and so on. But I do so during set hours that I control.

Scheduling your days and weeks like this ensures that you steadily accomplish both your short-term and long-term goals.

HOW TO ELIMINATE TIME WASTERS

The next thing you must do to boost your productivity and progress your company even faster is to eliminate interruptions and time wasters, which is *crucial* for you and your team to achieve peak performance.

Although often touted as a talent, multitasking actually hurts productivity. You might feel like you are accomplishing a lot when you're simultaneously answering e-mails, speaking to a customer, and training your employees, but you are invariably doing a less-than-acceptable job at each, and each task is taking longer than it should.

You simply cannot accomplish anything meaningful if you're constantly disrupted. Research states that it takes you seven minutes to regain concentration once you've been interrupted. Because seven minutes seems like a long time, let's say it takes only two minutes to regain your focus. Even at this reduced number, you'll lose 20 minutes of task-completion time for every 10 interruptions. Multiply that by 250 work days, and you're losing 83 hours each year.

Scheduling your days as I explained previously significantly helps avoid interruptions. For example, let's say you have a meeting at 3:00; you are not going to get interrupted at 3:10 because you are in that meeting. Because most of the meetings you set will be with yourself (e.g., to complete a project), you need to treat these meetings as seriously as if you were meeting with someone important. You wouldn't interrupt a meeting with the CEO of a large company who is seeking to acquire your company to pick up the phone, reply to an e-mail, or answer an employee's question, would you?

Scheduling your day down to the minute and refusing to allow interruptions during your meetings will get others in the habit

of not interrupting you and not wasting your time. The following text contains some other methods for avoiding the constant
interruptions and time wasters that reduce your productivity.

Eliminating Got-a-Minute Culture

Many entrepreneurs and business owners are frequently interrupted by employees saying, "Hey, got a minute?" for a question
they have. You must eliminate this got-a-minute culture. These
questions interrupt you and others in your company and are
rarely emergencies.

They also prevent important tasks from getting done in
a timely manner. With the ease of contacting provided by the
instant messaging (IM) capabilities in many businesses, this problem has been exacerbated even more in recent years. So, what
should you do?

Have your employees document each of their got-a-minute
questions, thoughts, or ideas, and hold periodic (perhaps weekly)
meetings to discuss these issues.

An added bonus of refusing to accept got-a-minute
questions—particularly from your direct reports—is that your
employees will be forced to work things out themselves. This
will help them grow as employees and increase their job satisfaction by making them feel more important.

You should also encourage your employees to follow the
same five-step productivity system you learned previously. By
breaking down their projects into smaller chunks, they will
think about the project and thus discover many of the questions
they might have in completing their projects. By documenting each of the questions and having one meeting with you (or
their direct supervisor) to answer them, you'll realize significant
time savings.

Of course, this means you can't have an open door policy, in which employees are comfortable walking into your office with questions. A lot of managers and business owners don't realize that it's perfectly ok to shut your door and get work done. Additionally, it sets a good example for others. A good idea is to set certain times of the week (e.g., one to three 30-minute blocks that you schedule on your calendar) when you *do* keep your door open and allow employees to come in with questions.

Unplug Your Phone

The next way to reduce interruptions is to stop answering unexpected phone calls.

Unless the call is expected call, don't take it. There are exceptions, of course: A prospective client that you need to close, or a call from your spouse or child. Other than that, however, you can't take the call or it will kill your productivity.

It's extremely hard to do this at first, as most of us are in the habit of picking up our phone immediately when it rings. One way to help is to turn off your ringer, or even pull your phone cord out (if you're working at a desk with a traditional phone).

Schedule one to three 15- to 30-minute blocks on your calendar each day to check and respond to voicemails. After listening, you can e-mail the caller to establish a set time for the callback. This avoids a game of phone tag and allows you to manage and control your phone on your schedule without interrupting your work on other key projects in your strategic plan.

Stop the Social Chit-Chat

Another crucial way to eliminate time interruptions and wasters is to stop the social chitchat, such as joking with employees, talking about last night's sports game or TV show, or gossiping about what's going on around the office.

Although it is critical for you to bond with your employees, you should schedule this as well, perhaps by holding office lunches, parties, or other types of informal get-togethers. Don't let social chit-chat interrupt your or your employees' days.

Although it might be considered a bit of a cop-out, feel free to work offsite some days. This helps you avoid social chit-chat and got-a-minute meetings. Remember that one of your key goals as the business owner is to allow the company to run without you. Working offsite on occasion can show you whether your business can in fact run without your involvement and help you find ways to improve it if it cannot.

Improving E-mail Management

The vast majority of business owners and employees spend way, way, *way* too much time writing and checking e-mails.

Consider this data from The Radicati Group, which researches e-mail usage: In 2011, the average person working at a corporation sent 33 e-mails and received 58 legitimate and 14 spam e-mails per day. Even if it only takes one minute to read, and three minutes to compose and send the average e-mail, that's 157 minutes per day, 654 hours per year, or 16 weeks spent checking e-mail!

This is far too much usually unproductive time. You need to manage your own and your employees' e-mail usage. The first step in doing so is to create *e-mail standards*.

One e-mail standard, albeit a strict one, to consider is to only send e-mails that you would put in the mail. Encourage employees to ask themselves: Is this e-mail *so important* that you would take the time to print it, put in an envelope, pay for postage, and go to the post office or postal box to mail it?

In most cases, you would avoid sending most e-mails based on this standard. Therefore, the first standard you must create in your company is what constitutes an acceptable e-mail.

Although you might not print and mail one e-mail to an employee, you might wait until you have 5 or 10 e-mails for the person and then send them as one physical letter.

Therefore, a second policy you should implement is to have your employees wait and combine multiple e-mails into one e-mail. This will dramatically cut down on the time needed for e-mail management in your company.

Likewise, you should have standards about how quickly someone should reply to an e-mail. Should it be within the hour, the day, or the next 48 hours? I personally hate when someone replies to my e-mails immediately. It tells me they are not being productive because I know they are not working on whatever project they should have been working on to reply to my e-mail.

Once again, you should set the standard, which should be based on your calendar. As you've done with returning phone calls, set one to three 15- to 30-minute blocks in your day during which you send and reply to e-mails.

This will keep e-mail from interrupting your day and will train your team and others to e-mail you less because they know they won't receive an instant reply. It will also allow you to reply to e-mails more quickly because you will process e-mails more efficiently when you know you have just 30 minutes to clean out your inbox.

Another key e-mail management technique is to keep your inbox clean. Seeing lots of e-mails in your inbox tends to produce a stressful, uneasy feeling. Conversely, you will have a very energetic feeling when you see an empty inbox.

You must implement e-mail filtering to accomplish this. Specifically, only e-mails from pre-approved people (e.g., employees, key customers or vendors, etc.) should go into your inbox. You could also set up other priority folders; for example, automatically filter messages from clients so they go into priority client e-mail folders. These are the e-mails (e.g., those in your inbox and priority folders) you will check one to three times per day. Other e-mails should go into a different folder (or multiple folders) that are lower priority. I label my main folder of this nature "Not Critical." Check these e-mails quickly and only once per day to maximize your productivity.

If an e-mail requires too much time to consider and reply, you may not be able to complete it within the time scheduled on your calendar for e-mail. In such a case, move the e-mail to a different folder (I call this my "To Deal With" folder) and schedule a future time on your calendar to handle it.

Finally, you should opt out of spam e-mails and e-mail newsletters that do not provide value. You need to periodically purge those e-mails. Just unsubscribe and don't deal with the clutter.

Managing your e-mail in the ways outlined above requires great discipline—but the rewards of massively increasing your productivity are worth it.

How to Hold Effective Meetings

Improving your meetings' effectiveness is another quick and easy way to enhance your overall company's productivity and performance.

Most companies spend far too much time in unnecessary meetings, meetings that last too long, or meetings that don't produce results. However, we all know that meetings are critical to solving issues and getting the team to work together more effectively. By following the tips in the following text, you'll be able to get your team together and produce the desired results.

First, only meet *when necessary*. Many questions can be resolved more efficiently through e-mail or other means rather than a meeting.

Second, keep your meetings to a *strict time limit*. Meetings that last more than one hour lose steam and focus. As such, limit your meetings to one to two hours at an absolute maximum.

Third, ensure you have a *set agenda* and *goal* for the meeting's outcome.

Fourth, unless the primary reason for the meeting is for social interaction, your meetings *shouldn't include food*. Food causes meetings to start late because you are waiting for it, and it unnecessarily extends meetings because your employees are having fun and thus want to spend more time in the meeting. This is usually *not* the meeting's goal.

Fifth, set the example by being punctual to meetings, which will force others to be punctual. You'll be able to start the meeting on time, and no one will be waiting for others to arrive. It also teaches everyone to be respectful of you and your other employees' time.

The sixth and final best practice for meetings is to ensure you have effective post-meeting follow-ups. Assign someone responsibility for documenting the key meeting points and creating to-do assignments with deadlines.

Follow these steps and you will spend less time in your meetings, which will be much more productive.

How to Achieve More by Doing Less

The final way to improve your productivity is to delegate as much as possible.

As company owner, you need to focus only on the items that add the most value to your organization. In general, these are the things that you, and *only* you, are capable of doing. You should delegate the rest.

Of course, you need a way to determine what the key things are on which you should be spending your time. Consider the Pareto Principle, or the 80/20 rule, which states that 20 percent of one thing (e.g., your customers) yields 80 percent of results (e.g., total company sales). In the case of your focus, the Pareto Principle says that 20 percent of your efforts yield 80 percent of the results you achieve. Therefore, the key is to identify what this 20 percent of your work is and do more of it (and delegate the 80 percent).

Identifying Your Top 20 Percent

The first way to determine which 20 percent of work you do yields 80 percent of the results is to think back. What were the most important projects you completed last year that propelled your company forward? Your answers will include the types of projects that belong in your top 20 percent and which you should continue to do.

The second way to determine your top tasks to perform is to review your to-do list and consider the following questions when reviewing each item:

- Does that activity really *add value* to your company?
- Are you *really great* at performing that task?
- Is there *somebody else who can do better, as well as, or nearly as well as you* at completing the task?

Finally, a great way to determine which tasks are *not* in your top 20 percent is to keep a running list of low-value tasks. To begin, you cannot be performing tasks that have a low dollar value. For example, you can't do work yourself that you could hire someone to do for $10 an hour.

As you go through your days, write down all tasks you perform that fall into this category. Common low dollar value tasks that business owners perform include:

- Mailing letters (including printing out envelopes and affixing postage)
- Sending faxes
- Ordering office supplies
- Managing vendors and paying invoices

Use these steps to determine the lowest value uses of your time and the highest value uses. The next step in the process is to delegate the lowest value uses to others.

Go to www.startatend.com to download a worksheet to identify low value uses of your time.

FIVE STEPS TO EFFECTIVELY DELEGATE

It is often hard at first for some entrepreneurs and business owners to delegate because they want to control everything themselves. However, to achieve your end vision, you must delegate. Consider Steve Jobs. He clearly didn't create the prototype for the iPod, nor did he manage the manufacturing, marketing, or customer service. Neither did Bill Gates. He clearly didn't write the code for all of Microsoft's products. Neither did Sir Richard Branson. How could Branson possibly manage nearly 50 companies at once without delegation?

The fact is this: Delegating tasks to others can save you a great deal of time and allow you to focus that time on the highest value-added tasks. However, when done incorrectly, delegating results in things not getting done or getting done poorly, which is when you end up expending more time and energy than you have.

This is why it's critical to delegate properly. Using the following steps will help you do so. Note that these steps are similar to the project management steps discussed in Chapter 5.

1. Identify the Right Person for Delegation

This person might be an employee of your company or an outsourced individual or firm. The right person is the one who has the requisite skill set to do the task and the ability to complete the project within the appropriate timeline.

Your employees should maintain daily and weekly to-do lists. This way, you can review those lists to identify which employees have the ability to tackle the project to be delegated.

2. Clearly Define the Project

The next step is to clearly define the task, the deliverables, the completion date, and why the project needs to be done. If you rush through this step and simply say, "do this by this date," you will get poor results.

For example, when I create a new product, there are a series of tasks I need to delegate to launch it. These include:

- Developing a logo and other graphic design elements for the product
- Creating a webpage detailing the product
- Developing an order form to sell the product
- Creating the system to deliver the product to the buyer after purchase

- Training the customer service team to answer questions about the product
- Writing advertisements to promote the product online
- Creating and managing online advertising campaigns for the product

Because I launch new products often, I have developed systems for each of these steps so they are completed quickly and consistently each time. Within my systems documents and when I first delegated the completion of these items, however, I needed to clearly define each project.

For example, for the first project (developing a logo and other graphic design elements for the product), I defined the project as follows:

- The date in which the logo or graphic design needed to be completed
- The format in which I needed the designs (e.g., GIF versus JPG files)
- The purpose of the designs (to promote the product and what the product was for)
- The intended audience for the product and the look and feel I was seeking (along with samples of other logos and graphic designs I liked and thought were relevant)
- My budget for completing the project (when assigned to a contractor)

Without such direction, it's obvious I would have set the project up for failure because the person to which I delegated wouldn't have had the information required to do a quality job. However, by planning and defining the project, success in delegating the project skyrockets.

3. Discuss the Plan of Action or How the Task Can Be Accomplished

Next, you need to discuss the plan of action: Specifically, how the person charged with completing the task can accomplish it.

Of key importance here is that you don't want to delegate a *task* (e.g., fax this report today), but rather a *process* (e.g., fax all the reports I have for now on). Therefore, even when delegating a seemingly simple task such as sending faxes, you need to discuss the plan. For example, how often do you need reports faxed? How quickly must they be faxed once you create them? What must be done after sending the fax? (Confirm receipt? Shred document?)

You want to spend time detailing and documenting how the delegated task should be performed.

4. Have Them Repeat Back the Plan

Next, have the person to whom you delegate repeat the task and deliverables back to you to ensure their complete comprehension. Most people will nod and say, "Yes, I get it"—that is, until you ask them to repeat your directions back, and they get them wrong. Have the person repeat all of your directions back to you until the directions are right.

5. Monitor Progress and Provide Feedback (Longer-Term Tasks)

When you delegate a task that will take more than one or two days, you need to monitor its progress and provide feedback. Ideally, you identified project milestones or checkpoints to ensure the project stays on track when initially discussing the plan.

To ensure projects are completed properly, mark those milestones on your calendar and monitor that results are delivered on time. If they are not, be sure to immediately alert the worker that he or she has fallen behind. Meet with the worker periodically to provide feedback and guidance.

6. Evaluate Performance

The final step to effective delegation is to evaluate performance. Most entrepreneurs and business owners skip this critical step and suffer as a result. Here's why: If somebody does a B+ job the first time they perform a task that you delegate, how do you think they'll perform the next time they do it?

Are they going to magically do an A+ job the next time? No. In fact, the next time they will do a B+ or lower job because they think that their B+ job is good enough. This is why providing feedback and evaluating performance allows you to get the best results from those to whom you delegate.

Even if they did a great job, you need to explain *why* they did a great job so that they know how to repeat this performance in the future. You need to explain if there was room for improvement. People generally appreciate slightly negative feedback versus no feedback at all. So, explain the good and the bad, and you'll get increasingly better results on the tasks you delegate to that person.

Finally, you need to understand and accept that it will often take at least twice as long to delegate a repeating task the first time as it would to do it yourself. However, once you delegate something successfully, it will be off your plate forever.

You must also accept that many delegated tasks may not get done as well as if you did them yourself. Although this isn't acceptable for some areas of your business (e.g., providing a service to a customer), for others (e.g., reordering supplies, completing paperwork), good enough is good enough.

Effective delegation makes you replaceable, and although it sounds a bit strange, this is what you want. It allows you to spend time growing—rather than simply maintaining—your business. You can spend less time working and take real vacations. It also makes your business attractive to buyers, which is particularly important if your end vision is to sell your company.

In this chapter, you learned productivity techniques that will allow you to achieve much more in much less time. Armed with these techniques, you can now spend your time on the highest value-added tasks and projects, which will allow you to achieve significant progress each week.

In the next chapter, I will teach you a related way to increase your company's sales and profits and progress toward your end vision much faster: by becoming a better leader. The techniques I will share with you will allow you to better motivate and improve the productivity of your workforce. Then both you and your team will become a well-oiled, high-production machine.

CHAPTER 12

BECOMING A BETTER LEADER

In the last chapter, you learned techniques to boost your productivity. If you can boost your productivity by 100 percent, or even just 20 percent or 40 percent, you will see a significant impact on your bottom line. What if you were able to see such productivity increases in each of your employees? Then you could see exponential increases to your bottom line. You'll also realize your financial metric and business asset goals that much faster.

One way to increase the productivity of your employees is to teach them the productivity techniques you learned in Chapter 11, and I encourage you to do just that. The other way to increase their productivity is to better motivate, train, and lead them.

Great leaders make all the difference. In sports, it's obvious what a great coach can do. Vince Lombardi, who led the Green Bay Packers to five NFL championships and two Super Bowl victories, is a great example of this. Later, in his first year coaching the Washington Redskins, he led them to their first winning season in more than a decade.

In business, we also see the impact of great leaders such as Tony Hsieh, who took the helm of online shoe retailer Zappos .com from founder Nick Swinmurn. Under Hsieh's leadership, the company grew from $1.6 million in sales in 2000 to more than $1 billion in sales in 2009.

Great leaders in both sports and business follow a similar blueprint. I lay out this blueprint, and the specific tactics great leaders use in the following text. Learn and use these tactics and you will achieve more success faster.

MOTIVATING YOUR EMPLOYEES

Through many years of research, trial and error, and working with companies of all sizes in numerous industries, I have identified 16 critical ways to motivate your employees. Learn these techniques and adapt as many as possible in your business.

1. Make Employees Feel They Are Doing Something Meaningful

A recent survey by BNET (which is now part of CBS MoneyWatch) asked the question, "What motivates you at work?"

The results showed that *doing something meaningful* is more important than money or recognition to your employees. Twenty nine percent of respondents said that doing something meaningful was the most motivating thing about work. Money motivated 25 percent, and recognition 17 percent.

Therefore, the number one way to motivate your team—your employees—is to make them feel that they are doing something meaningful. Now, if your vision is to alleviate poverty, as Kiva's is, getting your employees to feel like they are doing something meaningful is pretty easy. This might not seem quite as simple for the typical for-profit company. But this, too, is relatively straightforward. As discussed earlier, establishing your company's vision and goals—particularly involving your employees in creating them—will motivate them to achieve these objectives and help them feel that they are doing something meaningful.

Be sure to involve your employees in creating your company's vision (with your guidance, of course) and make them a part of establishing the goals in your business plan.

2. Effectively Communicate and Share Information

As discussed, all employees must clearly understand and support the company's vision, values, strategy, plans, and goals. You also must consistently share new information to ensure that your employees make good decisions.

You must always let employees know how the organization is progressing toward achieving goals. Setting KPIs and posting the associated KPI results monthly will allow you to achieve this.

The best example I've ever seen about how to communicate the results of goals and objectives was something I did in elementary school. When I was in third grade, my school held a canned food drive and stated our goal was to collect a certain amount: 1,000 cans of food.

Students would bring in cans every day and someone would count them. The school posted a chart in the front hallway that showed our progress. It allowed us to easily see how close we were to reaching our goal, which inspired each of us to bring in more canned food until we had collectively reached it.

As simple as it sounds, this chart was a highly effective way of communicating the results of our goal and our progress toward achieving it. However, few companies use such a proven mechanism.

You also must publicly acknowledge and reward the individuals who make contributions that help the company achieve its goals. Appreciation will keep your team motivated, so definitely recognize those employees who've accomplished tasks that have kept the organization on track.

3. Give Employees Clear Job Descriptions and Accountability

As initially discussed in Chapter 9, it is critical that you give each of your employees clear job descriptions and accountability. It's not enough to just state each role's responsibilities; rather, you must specify the expected results and tasks. For example, the customer service manager's described role might be to handle all inbound customer service calls. Their expected *results*, however, might be to answer all calls within 15 seconds or less, resulting in 90 percent customer satisfaction in telephone follow-up service. Only by specifying roles and expected results and accountability can you get what you want from each employee.

I heard a wonderful story in a presentation by Zappos CEO Tony Hsieh about an employee who really understood not only her job description but her total accountability.

Hsieh described the situation involving a customer who purchased a new pair of boots for her husband. In a tragic turn of events, the boots arrived the day after her husband died in a car accident, so the woman called Zappos and wanted to return the shoes. The Zappos customer service representative accepted the return right away. She didn't just let the woman return the shoes; she sent condolence flowers to the customer, who told her friends and family what Zappos had done for her at the funeral.

Zappos created a customer for life in this instance. This employee had a very clear job description and very clear decision-making authority regarding it. She obviously understood the organization's values and standards and made the right decision based on these values.

4. Give and Receive *Ongoing* Performance Feedback

You cannot comment only when things go wrong, which is unfortunately what most leaders and managers seem to do. You must provide feedback and comments when things go *right*, as well.

When things do go wrong, don't blame. You want to replace *who* questions with *how* questions. For example, rather than saying, "Who screwed this up?" say, "How could we improve this process or avoid this in the future?"

Official employment performance reviews are critical techniques that you as a leader can use to maximize the productivity and performance of your employees. We discuss these in more detail later in this chapter.

5. Have—and *Show*—Faith and Trust in Your Team

Most humans have relatively fragile self-esteem. If you don't believe your employees can do something, they won't believe they can either, and they won't do it. You must have faith in them. You can't just *say* you have faith: you need to *show* you do to enhance their confidence in their ability.

To achieve this, give your employees some autonomy to make decisions. Let them take ownership of challenging projects and decide how to complete them. Although it can be a challenge for almost any manager, you must let them fail sometimes and not get angry about it.

A lot of people suffer from low self-esteem because they did something wrong in their life or career. After all, who hasn't *ever* made a mistake? They likely heard early in their lives—probably from someone above them—that they messed something up or they weren't very good at something. They've carried these statements and beliefs with them ever since.

You have the power to turn this around by allowing your employees to fail at times without getting angry and by assuring them that you truly believe they can do whatever it is they've set out to do. You need to emphasize your team members' strengths and praise them often. By doing so, you'll give them confidence to build their self-esteem, thereby making them much more engaged and effective team employees.

6. Listen to, Focus on, and Respect Your Employees' Needs

You've likely heard this before, but it's worth repeating that in leadership, listening is more important than speaking. I love this quote: "Questions unite. Answers divide." Asking questions of your team will get them to participate; dictating the answers will cause them to tune out.

One of the seven habits in Stephen Covey's acclaimed book *The 7 Habits of Highly Effective People* is: "Seek first to understand than to be understood." Do not assume that you know the answers; listen to others in an attempt to find them. Always try to understand what other people want or need before you begin to outline your own objectives. It's always a good move to focus less on how you feel and more on how your employees feel. What are their major concerns? What do they like? What do they dislike? The more you can determine these things about your team and treat them well, the more highly motivated the team will be, and the better they will perform.

7. Provide Recognition to Worthy Employees

Recognition is an amazing motivator. Adrian Gostick and Chester Elton authored a book called *The Carrot Principle* in which they discuss a study of more than 200,000 employees that they conducted over a 10-year period. The study showed that the most successful managers provided their employees with frequent and effective recognition. In fact, they found that managers realized significantly better business results when they offered employees recognition in the form of constructive praise rather than monetary rewards.

Be sure to recognize your employees. At Growthink, we have weekly company conference calls. During them, Jay Turo (my cofounder at Growthink) and I acknowledge those employees who recently did something exceptional. We also continually seek to provide recognition to employees in the form of small gifts based on the employee's personal needs. For example, one employee hadn't been able to spend enough quality time with her husband, so after she successfully completed a job, we gave her a gift certificate to a nice restaurant so she could enjoy a romantic dinner with her husband. For other employees, the gifts may be something they can do with their kids.

The key is to recognize your employees for their efforts and determine the best method with which to motivate them (e.g., a small gift relating to something they cherish, public acknowledgement, etc.).

8. Provide Fair Compensation and Pay for the Performance You Seek

Of course, although recognition is the most important way to motivate your employees, monetary payment is still critical to motivate and satisfy them. The keys to providing monetary payments are as follows.

First, you must pay a wage that employees believe is fair compensation. Second, you must pay for performance whenever possible. This does not mean 100 percent contingent compensation. It means that you set expectations for base pay while also providing bonuses and clearly defining success. This will compel employees to strive to achieve the goals you have outlined.

9. Foster Innovation

Effective leaders seek new ideas and opinions from their employees. Nothing is more motivating for a particular team member than to work on an idea that they or a teammate developed.

Managers must realize that the vast majority of innovations come from front-line employees. They come from the people who are manufacturing your products or designing your services, who are interfacing with customers, and who are solving problems on a daily basis. As such, innovation must be encouraged.

This approach provides a win–win situation. Employees enjoy coming up with new ideas, and you benefit from implementing these ideas. Employees are incredibly motivated when they feel that management is truly listening to them.

A simple suggestion box can be a highly effective way to propel this kind of interaction and collaboration. Proper communication in this instance is to say both on the box and verbally to your team that the suggestion box's goal is to share everyone's ideas for company improvement.

10. Establish Fair Company Policies That Support the Company's Goals

Developing fair company policies that adequately support the company's goals will motivate your employees even more. For example, you cannot treat attending a seminar as a personal day if you want to encourage continuous learning. Rather, ensure your policies and practices encourage employee feedback, collaboration, decision-making, and so on.

Likewise, if you want to encourage creativity, requiring your employees to wear suits every day and holding meetings in staid conference rooms will not yield the results you seek.

11. Get Ongoing Input from Employees

As discussed previously, you want to invite your employees to help set goals so that they really buy into them. Seek employee input on key decisions and plans on an ongoing basis.

Understand that as the leader, you will make the ultimate decisions and plans. Even if you don't follow your employees' advice or take their suggestions verbatim, however, the very act of soliciting their feedback will give you more information and ideas and will make them feel involved.

12. Manage, but Don't *Micro*manage

Employees do not like to be micromanaged. It's disempowering. It's therefore important to distinguish the difference between checking in and checking up on your employees. Checking *in*, for example, would be meeting with your employees to learn their progress on completing a project and offering guidance, advice, and support to help them better finish the task. Checking *up* would be solely asking about whether an employee finished a task. The difference is one of working *with* your employees versus simply demanding results.

Likewise, when managing, don't dictate every detail of how to complete a project. Remember, employees can't grow and gain new skills if you're telling them exactly what to do for every project they work on. They need a sense of autonomy to feel that they're succeeding.

13. Encourage Teamwork

Although every employee should have specific tasks for which they are responsible, having employees work in formal or even informal teams will encourage them to become more engaged with their work. Being part of a cohesive team fosters a sense of belonging and community that will allow you to get the most from your employees.

As you saw in the sample Gantt charts in Chapter 5, most projects you complete will require input from several employees within your organization. Encourage these employees to work as a team rather than a collection of individuals to complete these projects. The easiest way to do this is to set up an initial meeting for the team, refer to them as a team, and give them enough autonomy (once again, don't dictate precisely how they must do things) so they act like a team.

14. Modify Your Management Approach for Different Types of Employees

Great leaders let the employees they're managing dictate the management approaches they use. Some employees may need or desire more handholding and coaching, whereas others will want or require less. It's important to think about each key employee and determine the best way to lead him or her. Clearly, a new employee is going to need more handholding, whereas an older, superstar employee may just want you to check in once in a while.

The way you manage each employee doesn't always depend on their age, experience, role, and so on, but should be based on their personality and preferences. By meeting with your employees periodically, you can better understand their needs and manage accordingly.

15. Give Employees Opportunities for Personal Growth

Because people who get the chance to grow their skills and expertise take more pride in their jobs, you want to encourage employees in your organization to gain new skills. You can do this in many ways, such as providing on-the-job training and other opportunities to teach your employees new skills (we'll cover this in more detail in the next section).

16. Fire People When Needed

The final technique for motivating your team is to fire people when needed. Underperformers can kill an organization; they can become cancers. When other employees see these individuals getting away with underperformance, then they start to underperform. Therefore, firing—as long as you explain to your team why people were fired—can actually motivate your employees.

We will discuss specific firing tactics later in this chapter.

Go to www.startatend.com to download a checklist to ensure you continue to properly motivate your employees.

TRAINING AND MENTORING YOUR EMPLOYEES

As discussed previously, training employees both formally and informally will motivate them to perform better. Because it also gives them the skills to perform better, it is truly a situation that benefits everyone involved.

Motivational speaker and trainer Brian Tracy tells a great story about training. As a young man, Tracy went to work at a sales organization where he initially did poorly. He had trouble getting appointments and closing deals. He noticed that most of his coworkers were having the same problems.

However, Tracy saw one salesperson in the organization that seemed to have figured everything out. This guy always had appointments. He was always closing new deals. As a result, this individual was always the company's number one salesperson.

Tracy went over to this salesperson and said, "Hey, you think you can help me get better at my sales skills?" The top performer proceeded to train and teach him, and Tracy ended up becoming a phenomenal salesperson. Here's the most interesting part, however: When Tracy later asked the salesperson if anyone had asked him to train them before, he said no.

This story conveys several important points about improving your leadership skills. First, the leader of that organization should have recognized this top performer's excellent skills and had him train the other employees. Because a leader's role is to help people improve, taking this approach would have made the entire company much more successful.

Brian Tracy also showed great resourcefulness in asking his colleague for help. Most people wouldn't, and as evidenced by his story, hadn't taken that initiative. Importantly, because most of your employees won't take the same initiative Tracy did, you must encourage employee mentoring. Consider giving better employees monetary and nonmonetary incentives to do so.

The final point of the story was that the top performer was good at sales because he had been trained at a Fortune 500 company. However, any organization—even if you're not a Fortune

500 company—must have training as a key initiative. You can't just put employees in roles and expect them to excel. You must show them exactly what excelling looks like.

There are three core types of training that you can give your employees:

1. On-the-job training, which can be both formal and informal
2. Coaching and mentorship
3. Discipline training

The first of these, on-the-job training, is task-specific. For example, this might be how to provide customer service at your organization, how to produce widgets, or how to prepare a certain type of report.

Formal on-the-job training usually consists of structured courses with a teacher, a DVD, a CD, or a manual. The informal approach is essentially to watch and learn. For example, in one of my first jobs, auditing the circulations of trade magazines, there were no structured courses for me to take. Rather, I simply followed an experienced auditor for four weeks and learned from watching the auditor perform the work.

You should formalize your training whenever possible because formalized training:

1. Forces you to think through procedures much more thoroughly, which often helps identify flaws and ways to improve.
2. Makes it much easier and faster for new hires to learn your systems.
3. Ensures consistency in training.
4. Makes it easier for an outsider, such as a consultant, to

come in and quickly understand what's going on, and therefore help you improve your business.

5. Adds a lot of value to your business and makes it more sellable and at a higher price. Businesses that are systematized are easier to run by a new owner. They are much more valuable and easier to sell, and they sell at a premium price.

Finally, role-playing can also be a great form of on-the-job training to ensure employees really understand the company's vision and values and what is expected of them.

As the leader, you want to ask lots of "what if"? questions to train the team. For example: What should a person behind a cash register do if a customer receives a phone call on their mobile phone and starts sobbing? Should they leave the cash register and help the person?

Asking these "what if"? role-playing questions can be part of or go beyond the formal training. They work because they ensure that employees understand your organization's vision and values, and can make the right decisions.

The second type of training is *coaching and mentorship*, which is the process of giving employees advice and assistance in solving their problems and improving their performance. This aspect of training can also be formal or informal. A formal program would involve having 30-minute coaching sessions once a month, whereas informal coaching might include 15- to 30-minute meetings as needed.

There are three keys to effective coaching and mentorship:

First, you must listen more than you speak. Ask probing questions and listen attentively to the answers. *Second*, even if you think you're taking your time, *slow down*. You are coaching and mentoring employees because they don't have your skills and abilities. Do not rush them; realize it will take time for them to improve. And *third*, as a leader, mentor, and coach, avoid criticizing and getting frustrated. You can give negative feedback, but you need to focus on how to improve. For example, if your website developer uploaded a page to your website with typos on it, explain that they could avoid such a problem in the future if they spell-checked pages beforehand.

The third and final type of training is *discipline training*, which includes helping improve a specific skill set by partaking in activities such as attending a seminar on improving sales techniques, getting a DVD on how to better use a computer program, or reading a book about a specific manufacturing process.

To really improve your organization and lead it to success, you need to create a culture of learning and training. You must make sure your employees know that you support their continuing education and skill development, and show this support by providing funding for these endeavors.

CONDUCTING EMPLOYEE PERFORMANCE REVIEWS

Employee performance reviews are traditionally defined as a method by which a manager evaluates an employee's job performance. This definition follows the old saying that you can't improve what you can't measure, which is true. By measuring an employee's performance and providing feedback, you can improve the employee's performance. However, giving and improving employee performance is just one of two key aspects of an employee performance review.

The second key aspect, which is just as—if not more—important, is to ensure that the employee's objectives are clear and consistent with the company's objectives and goals. Even if employees are doing an amazing job completing their day-to-day tasks, these tasks don't have much value if they aren't congruent with the company's strategic plans and goals. This is therefore the ideal opportunity to confirm that your employees' goals are aligned with the company's.

Performance reviews also allow you to reward your employees or have them improve their performance, specifically by encouraging them to achieve their objectives more quickly and effectively. Remember what we learned earlier in the chapter: Rewards do not have to be monetary to motivate. They can be as simple as telling someone "great job" or giving public recognition. The goal is to go through their performance with them and help them *do* a great job and then recognize them if they're doing well.

According to Mike Carden, cofounder of the employee performance software Sonar6, most employees actually enjoy their reviews. As Mike told me, "It's sort of like playing golf. Even if you didn't play great, you want to know your score at the end."

Even if they didn't do a great job, employees *do* want to know how they did. This is why you need to ensure you complete the employee performance reviews, however time-consuming and difficult the process can sometimes be. From your perspective, performance reviews should achieve the positive benefit of alleviating the frustration that ensues when employees don't accomplish key objectives. The reviews will allow you spot and improve performance.

The following are some best practices for employee performance reviews:

First, make sure your employees have specific goals and objectives to achieve. If they don't, it's very hard to judge their performance. It's not fair to judge an employee against criteria of which they were unaware.

Your review should focus on how the employee performed versus the goals and objectives. Discuss both the positives and negatives, and don't dwell too closely on the bad points. The goal is not to make the employee feel bad but rather to determine which tools, information, and guidance they need to achieve their goals during the next period. Your goal is to focus on finding the root cause of poor performance so you can take actions to fix it.

Make sure you not only look backward at how the employee performed in the last period, but look forward to the next period. You should help reevaluate and reset your objectives for that employee as appropriate, particularly if your organization's overall strategy or business plan has shifted.

Performance reviews should be part of an ongoing process. Rather than merely complete them annually, you should conduct them on a monthly basis. Although this might seem to need quite a bit of your time, the process should take no longer than 20 to 30 minutes to complete.

Annual reviews generally focus on "Here's how you are doing; should we give you a raise?" However, that shouldn't be the goal. The performance review's objective is to help make the employee more productive so you can lead a better organization that achieves all of its goals.

You conduct performance reviews to get the best out of your people. They shouldn't be intimidating critiquing sessions, but rather a way to ensure your employees are clear about—and remain focused on—their and the company's objectives. They are chances for everyone to concentrate on helping all team members achieve those objectives more successfully.

FIRING TACTICS

As mentioned previously, at some point you'll have to let some workers go. There will be times that you simply must fire employees.

You might be familiar with the saying "Hire slowly, fire quickly." When a certain member of your organization is clearly not working out, you need to get rid of them as swiftly as possible.

A single bad employee can have a detrimental effect on the whole organization. The entire company suffers when non-team players—people who don't embody the values of the company, believe in the vision, or work hard enough—are present. There's a very real danger that they'll bring others in your organization down to their level.

Firings are very tough decisions and stressful to handle; however, in certain cases, they are the only option. Most of the time, your employees will thank you and you will thank yourself later.

Although the situation will clearly differ somewhat from one organization and employee to another, the following are five steps to effectively firing an employee.

Step number 1 is to *ask if firing is truly necessary*. Did you give the employee any feedback on his or her performance so far, or provide him or her with an opportunity to change? If you didn't, it might not be necessary to fire them quite yet. Perhaps you need to spend more time with that employee, reset their objectives, and give them the opportunity to grow and perform better.

If, on the other hand, you've given ample chances to turn her or his performance around and it hasn't worked, the second step is to *act quickly*. Once you determine that firing is necessary, you must do it as soon as possible. The longer you tolerate a poor employee, the more stress it's going to cause you—and the longer other employees will have to endure the bad influence and the apparent lack of leadership on your part.

Third, you must *identify when and where you will handle the firing*. Ideally, you'll fire somebody earlier in the day or week, particularly when there aren't too many other employees around. Some business owners like to do it on Friday afternoons, whereas others prefer Monday morning. The key is to do it without delay.

Next, you must *be clear and concise.* You want employees to know that they're not being transferred or laid off temporarily. You need to say either *terminate, let you go,* or *fire.*

You must fire respectfully to avoid legal action and potential outbursts that will affect other employees. Therefore, you need to think it through a little. In doing so, a good idea is to role play the firing with a business partner, mentor, or colleague. This will help alert you to things that may go wrong and allow you to preempt them and be prepared for different scenarios. Once you do that, you must act decisively and concisely, and be very, *very* clear.

The final step to effectively firing an employee is to *tell the rest of your team right away,* ideally by calling a meeting. You must provide clarity on why the employee was fired so everyone knows why and doesn't repeat the mistakes that person made. You also don't want other employees to experience unmerited stress over losing *their* jobs. When you fire somebody, it should motivate the rest of your team. For example, if the fired employee wasn't embodying the company's vision, then other employees will understand the importance of the vision. Likewise, the firing should show employees that poor performance and behaviors will not be tolerated. Your better performers will appreciate this and the fact that you are holding your employees to a high standard.

Remember the old saying: "Hire slowly but fire quickly." Remember as well that firing—although always stressful and uncomfortable—will probably motivate the rest of your team in a good way. When done appropriately, the firing reiterates your company's vision and requirement that employees maintain high standards.

Leading any organization is hard work, and implementing each of the tactics outlined in this chapter will take some time. That's okay. Adopt one new tactic every other month, and by year's end, your team will be more motivated and producing twice as much as last year.

In the next chapter, I will present several multiplier tactics. These are strategies that, when added to the ideas and tactics you have learned so far, can multiply your results even further. You'll grow your revenues and profits even more and reach your end vision even faster.

CHAPTER 13

MULTIPLIER TACTICS

I have handed you proven strategies, ideas, and tactics that I have used for more than a decade in growing my own businesses and those of my clients. Follow them and I assure you that you'll achieve more success. However, I would be remiss if I didn't hand you the following tactics and strategies that have aided my own and other business owners' success over the years. I call these multiplier tactics because each has the ability to further multiply the positive results you will receive from developing and executing on your business plan.

For example, the following techniques will allow you to multiply your marketing success to generate more revenues. They will allow you to improve your systems to complete projects even faster and therefore boost profits. They will allow you to more quickly identify high-leverage projects, or those that you can complete quickly and see immediate returns. Each tactic on its own will boost your success, but when combined with your business plan and the other strategies we've discussed, they will allow you to quickly grow your sales and profits and progress even faster toward your end vision.

Consider employing these tactics now to reap immediate rewards, after you have executed on the other strategies I've shared with you to multiply your successes even further.

LEVERAGE THE PARETO PRINCIPLE THROUGHOUT YOUR BUSINESS

The first multiplier tactic is to leverage the Pareto Principle throughout your business. As discussed in Chapter 11, the Pareto Principle, or the 80/20 rule, states that 20 percent of one thing yields 80 percent of results.

For example, 80 percent of your sales might be produced by:

- 20 percent of your sales team
- 20 percent of your customers
- 20 percent of your products

Think about how this rule applies to your business. Do you have a certain customers who represent the majority of your revenues? If so, concentrate on identifying their characteristics and make a concerted effort to find more customers like them.

Do certain members of your sales team dominate? Determine why and what characteristics make them so successful so you can find new sales team members like them or train your other current sales team members to work like they do.

Do certain products or services comprise the majority of your sales? If so, consider creating more offerings like them and possibly dropping product lines that aren't performing. If these are limiting your resources, you can instead focus on the ones that *do* perform.

Bottom line: Identify the 20 percent of things throughout your business that produce the most results and do more of them. This is called *leverage*, and it can quickly boost your results.

DO MORE OF WHAT WORKS

I'm not sure whether the following story is true. However, I have seen many companies—including mine—use it very successfully.

There was once a young man who had just graduated from college with an engineering degree. He did what most of his classmates did and got a job as an engineer. Within the next few years he got married and had his first child, and then another child.

After working for the man for 20 years, he decided to start his own engineering consulting firm. Although business was slow at first, he built up his firm over the years. In fact, 30 years after founding his company, he was generating millions of dollars in annual revenues.

But then, at the age of 72, he died, and he left the business to his 71-year-old wife.

His wife had never run a business in her life. In fact, she spent most of her days at the country club golfing and dining with her friends.

Within a year, however, she had doubled the firm's profits.

How did she do it? Simple. She visited the company a week after her husband passed and sat down with the management team. She told them to do two things:

1. Make me a list of the five things that worked the *best* in the last 12 months
2. Make me a list of the five things that worked the *least* in the last 12 months

The list of things that worked included upselling current clients, getting new clients from partnerships they formed, and their program that hired and trained new sales reps. The things that didn't work included radio advertising, sponsoring trade shows, and a new service offering that just didn't catch on.

The widow made one demand: Do more of the five things that worked, and stop doing the five things that didn't work.

The management team listened. Within a year, the company's revenues and profits both doubled.

Yes, it's that simple. Your company should do more of the things that are proven to work and less of the things that haven't worked. Unfortunately, most business owners don't do this, and here's why: We've been told throughout our lives to improve our weaknesses and never quit, and we carry this lesson over to our businesses. So when something doesn't work, our first impression is typically to work on it or try to fix it.

However, that's generally not the best solution. A much more effective approach is to do more of what is already working. Why try to fix an unproven concept when you already have a winner?

For example, one of my clients was having success selling low-priced products. In doing so, they had built up a sizable base of customers. The client was also having success selling additional low-priced products to these customers.

Naturally, the client started thinking that he would be able to generate more sales and profits if he sold higher-priced products to his customers. Although his thinking was correct, that the higher-priced products would maximize sales and profits, each time my client launched a high-priced product, few of his customers purchased it.

He didn't give up, however, and kept trying to fix the problem, but he couldn't. The problem was solved when I told him that maybe his customers just couldn't afford the high-priced products and he should focus on creating many more low-priced products. We developed a system to allow my client to create new, low-priced products four times faster than before. His customers purchased the new low-priced products en mass, and the company's sales and profits grew by leaps and bounds.

When it comes to marketing, I always suggest that companies tweak and test new ideas because creating new profitable promotional vehicles can give you competitive advantage. This does mean working on ideas that fail at first to see if you can improve them. In most other areas, however, you should focus more on your winners.

Take out a pen and paper and:

1. Make a list of the five things that worked the best for you in the last 12 months
2. Make a list of the five things that worked the least for you in the last 12 months

And then make sure to add the five things that worked best to this year's business plan.

DEVELOP AN ADVISORY BOARD

An advisory board will help you grow your company. At the very least, it provides a sounding board and reality check to ensure you complete and fully execute on your business plan. Because advisors might have already encountered and solved the same challenges you face, they could provide a critical outside perspective.

Who or what are advisors? Advisors are successful people who you respect and who agree to help your company. They're generally successful or retired executives, business owners, service providers, professors, or others who could help you out. Advisors generally will not cost you any money because you don't pay them, although I do recommend giving them stock options to incentivize them to contribute as much as possible.

Advisors can help you in a variety of ways, such as:

Driving Operational Success. Having advisors with whom you can discuss key business matters as you grow your venture will help ensure you make the right decisions, particularly if they have encountered and dealt with the same challenges already in their companies and careers. These individuals can also give you an outside opinion on the opportunities you're considering pursuing in your business plan.

Making Connections. The successful individuals you choose as advisors will often have large, high-quality networks of individuals to whom they can introduce you. Likewise, the right advisors can connect you with key strategic partners, employees, and customers.

Enhancing Credibility. Having quality advisors also gives your company more credibility, which can help with gaining new customers, partners, and media mentions.

How to Build Your Board of Advisors

Keep in mind that you don't necessarily need to build a board of advisors; having just one mentor or advisor is certainly better than none. My experience has shown, however, that having several people to guide you in a board dynamic allows you to get better ongoing feedback and advice. Also, a larger board will give you access to more connections, experiences, and expertise.

To build your board of advisors, create a list of people you'd like to ask and contact them. Start by outlining your key goals when you're making this list. Are they:

- *Credibility?* Then a local or industry celebrity may work best, or someone with a lofty title or a professor.
- *Connections to capital?* A financial type, someone who has raised capital, or someone who has worked as a banker or investor might be best.
- *Connections to customers, strategic partners, distributors, and so on?* Then someone who has worked in the industry for many years would be an ideal choice.

- *Expertise in growing a successful business?* Someone who has reached goals that you would like to reach (e.g., grew a $50 million business, successfully sold their business, etc.) might be perfect for this. Likewise, someone who has a unique skill set in a certain discipline, such as sales management, could be great.

Overall, your list of prospective advisors will include successful people that can help. Some will be within your field or industry, whereas others will be outside of it. These individuals might be retired or current executives, business owners, consultants or professional service advisors, professors, and so on.

Leveraging Your Board of Advisors

Once you have built your board, hold periodic—either monthly or quarterly—meetings with your members to leverage them: to get them to make introductions, help solve operational challenges, give you feedback on your performance, help set future goals, and so on. Ideally, certain board members will also be available via e-mail or telephone to help answer questions between meetings.

BUILD NANOSYSTEMS FOR SYSTEMATIC IMPROVEMENTS

In Chapter 6 you learned how to create systems for your business. We explained that the four purposes of your systems included increased precision and consistency, time and money savings, scalability, and the ability to free your time and build business value.

To reap even more benefit from your systems, break them down further into nanosystems. As the name implies, *nanosystems* are very small systems; they result from taking your established systems, scrutinizing their details, and generating ideas for improving each detail.

In the following I map out how to create nanosystems and how doing so can increase your sales and profits.

As an example, let's say that your firm provides accounting services for small businesses. Your main challenge is to increase revenues and profits, which is generally going to be composed of three smaller challenges:

- Getting more clients
- Fully satisfying those clients
- Getting those clients to buy more from you

How will your accounting firm achieve this goal of increasing revenues and profits? The answer is to have a marketing system that includes the following four processes:

1. *Lead sourcing*: how your accounting firm gets new leads
2. *Lead conversion*: how your firm converts these leads into prospects (I'll discuss the difference between leads and prospects in more detail later)
3. *Prospect development and closing*: how your firm converts prospects into clients
4. *Fulfillment and upselling*: how your firm completes client work and upsells them on additional work they need

The next step is to determine what you are doing within each of these processes, what you are tracking, and where you can improve for each of the four processes.

Let's start with the first process: lead sourcing, which we define here as getting an individual to contact you (either via telephone, e-mail, visiting your website, etc.) because they have a possible interest in working with you.

Your current list of what you are doing may include:

- Getting referrals from customers
- Getting referrals from partners
- Newspaper advertising

Your current list of what you are tracking may include:

- How many leads you get each month

And your ideas for improvement may include:

- Trying new forms of promotions such as radio advertising, social media marketing, and direct mail
- Improving your customer referral program by offering rewards
- Better tracking of lead sources and which leads convert so you know which lead sources generate the most customers

I'll complete the process later, but I want you to understand the end result, so here it is: By breaking up and scrutinizing all the specific processes involved in the whole system, you will identify ways to massively improve performance.

Let's move on to the second process: Lead conversion, or converting an individual from a lead (someone who has gone to your website or called you) to a prospect (someone who has shown a more serious intent of buying from you).

Your current list of what you are doing may include:

- Fielding phone calls and e-mails from leads
- Routing them to your best salespeople

Your current list of what you are tracking may include:

- How many calls and e-mails you receive each month
- How many of these calls and e-mails become clients

And your ideas for improvement may include:

- Developing a better script to use when handling incoming phone inquiries
- Outsourcing incoming phone calls during off hours so leads can reach you at any time
- Improving the time delay from when the receptionist speaks to the lead and the lead speaks to your salesperson
- Identifying which salespeople perform best with which types of leads and routing accordingly

The third process to improve is prospect development and closing, or how your firm converts prospects into clients.

Your current list of what you are doing may include:

- Conducting initial needs analysis calls with prospects
- Preparing price proposals

Your current list of what you are tracking may include:

- How many proposals you give each month
- What percentage of proposals become clients

And your current list of ideas for improvement may include:

- Better training your salespeople
- Finding better salespeople
- Creating better sales scripts

- Improving the quality of proposal documents
- Better follow-up on prospects who initially reject proposals

The fourth and final process to improve is fulfillment and upselling, or how your firm completes client work and upsells them on additional work they need.

Your current list of what you are doing may include:

- Holding face-to-face meetings and calls
- Preparing key deliverables sent via e-mail and messenger

Your current list of what you are tracking may include:

- How satisfied your clients are
- Number and percentage of clients who repurchase the same service over time
- Number and percentage of clients who purchase additional services from you

And your current list of ideas for improvement may include:

- Having additional points of interaction with clients (e.g., extra meetings, video conferences) to build more rapport during engagements
- Bringing in a senior manager into all engagements to check work and provide additional insight to better satisfy clients
- Creating formal processes that require your staff to ask for referrals, testimonials, and additional work opportunities during client engagements
- Adding additional tracking to learn which staff members get the most referrals, testimonials, and additional work opportunities

By breaking up any process into smaller pieces and then scrutinizing each of the smaller pieces, it's simple to come up with *tons* of ideas for improvement. You will also identify new processes to add that further boost your profits and competitive advantage.

In fact, the problem quickly switches to an implementation issue, that is, "How do I start implementing all of the great ideas I came up with?"

Here I suggest putting all of the ideas, along with their category (which process they relate to) into an Excel spreadsheet. In a column next to each idea, rank the idea from 1 to 5, with 1 being an idea that can make the most significant and immediate impact on your bottom line and 5 being an idea that will take longer to implement or that may not impact your bottom line as much.

Then sort the ideas by rank. Finally, create a Gantt chart, as you learned to do in Chapter 5, showing which ideas you will start implementing first, next, and then last. The Gantt chart will allow you to see who is working on which idea and set a time frame for when you want to finish.

Following this systematization approach truly allows you to improve anything. Yes, it's a lot of work, but it's relatively fun work, and it always leads to success!

USE THE IMPROVEMENT MATRIX TO ENHANCE YOUR PRODUCTS AND SERVICES

The improvement matrix is a way of looking at your products and services and determining what you should improve upon and in what order.

Let me provide an example. Let's take a look at Sal. (Sal's actually my landscaper. He is great at what he does but he frustrates me to no end because he's such a bad marketer. I'd really like to help him improve this part of his business.) The first step is to identify what your customers find most important.

Because I'm a landscaping customer, Sal should survey me and his other customers on the 8 to 12 attributes of his business that I find most important. Sal might have chosen the following attributes to survey:

1. Quality of lawn mowing
2. Quality of plant trimming
3. Offers to do additional work (e.g., clean leaves from gutters)
4. Price
5. Value (fairness of price based on quality of service)
6. Ease of billing
7. Ease of communications with company
8. Professionalism of workers

For each attribute, he should ask customers, "How important are these attributes to you in your landscaping company?"

He could use a four-point scale as follows:

1—Not important

2—Somewhat important

3—Very important

4—Extremely important

The results may have looked like Figure 13.1.

As you can see, Sal's customers considered "quality of lawn mowing" and "ease of billing" to be the most important attributes. The least important attributes were "professionalism of workers" and "offers to do additional work."

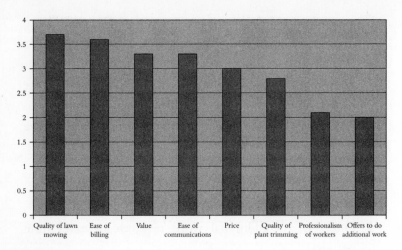

Figure 13.1   Importance of Key Attributes

The next question on Sal's survey should be: "How do you rate my performance on these attributes?"

He could use a four-point scale again as follows:

1—Poor

2—Fair

3—Very good

4—Excellent

Sal should judge responses to this performance question against how important the attributes are. The results may have looked like Figure 13.2.

As you can see from the chart, Sal's performance on attributes such as "value" is in line with what his customers consider important. However, Sal is vastly underperforming on the key attribute of "ease of billing." Additionally, he is overperforming on the less-important attribute of "professionalism of workers" (maybe Sal has his workers dress in formal uniforms, a move his customers deem unnecessary).

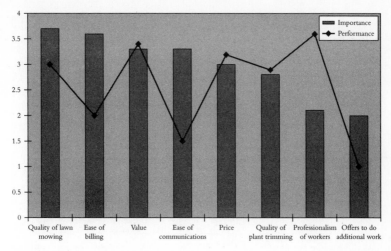

Figure 13.2   Importance vs. Performance on Key Attributes

So, what should Sal do? The first thing is to focus on improving his "ease of billing" because this will improve customer satisfaction. And if he is investing too much money and time in "professionalism of workers," he should consider reallocating those resources to improving "ease of billing."

It's easy to see the beauty of the chart, based on two simple sets of questions for customers, because it identifies the most important areas of your product or service to fix to better satisfy customers and gain competitive advantage.

Now, a final way to look at the performance chart is as a matrix. I call this the improvement matrix (see Figure 13.3).

The improvement matrix is simply a different way of looking at importance versus performance data. It plots the data and classifies each attribute into four quadrants:

1. *Underperforming (but okay):* you are underperforming in this area, but customers don't care much about it, so it's acceptable.
2. *Overperforming:* you are doing well in this area, but customers don't value it. You can keep doing what you're

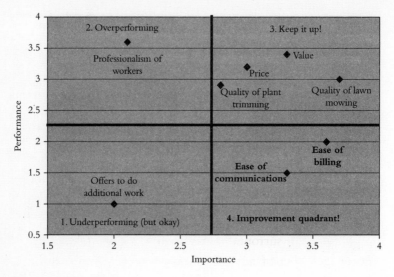

Figure 13.3　The Improvement Matrix

doing or consider allocating resources away from this area into a more important area.

3. *Keep it up:* these are areas that your customers care about in which you are doing well, so continue doing what you're doing.

4. *Improvement:* This quadrant is the one that most requires your attention. It shows those areas that customers find important but for which your performance is not up to speed. You *must* get better in these areas as soon as possible.

As you can see, the improvement matrix will alert you to the key areas of your product and service that you must improve. All it requires is a simple customer survey and plotting of the data, and you'll get results that have the potential to revolutionize your business. So do it!

HANG OUT WITH WINNERS

Success coach Jim Rohn said, "You are the average of the five people you hang around with most."

It's true. If you hang out with losers, you'll unfortunately be a loser. But if you hang out with winners, you'll become a winner, because winners have a different way of thinking. And winners—particularly other successful entrepreneurs and business owners with whom you should be spending time—have often already encountered and overcome the challenges you face in your business.

How do you surround yourself with winners? One way is to form a board of advisors as discussed previously. Another approach is to meet or seek winners out at networking events, or perhaps start a local Mastermind group where you and other business owners meet monthly to share what's working in your businesses and what challenges you face.

In addition to spending time with winning entrepreneurs and business owners in general, find ones who have already achieved what you'd like to achieve. For example, if your goal is to grow to $25 million in annual sales, spend time with someone who's already built a $25 million business because they will have great insight into what you need to do to achieve that same success.

The goal of this book is to help you develop a proven plan to follow to reach your end vision. In the earlier chapters, you crafted this vision and established your goals. You then developed specific marketing and human resource strategies and documented your strategic plan to follow. Then you learned how to make both you and your team more productive. Finally, in this chapter, you learned several ideas and approaches to multiplying your success even more. In giving you these ideas, I not only wanted you to receive immediate gains, but I wanted to show you that you can always be making incremental improvements to your business. By implementing these tactics into your strategic plan and committing to constant and ongoing improvements, your company will flourish and competitors will be left in the dust.

CONCLUSION

As you've learned throughout the pages of this book, the right business plan can transform your business. It can boost your sales and profits, and allow you to achieve the goals you had when you first launched or purchased your business.

However, your business plan can only do this if you complete it properly. Most important, you must start with the end. You must dream big about what you'd like your business to achieve. Once you have that crystal-clear vision, you can begin planning and reverse engineering it.

Remember to develop and document your vision from a customer perspective—what you are trying to do for your customers. Then document your vision from a business perspective—what you are trying to achieve financially, such as selling your business for $40 million within 5 years.

Once you develop your long-term vision, you must reverse engineer it by determining your annual, quarterly, and monthly goals. Although your plans can and will change over time, each of these periodic goals will move your company closer to its ultimate end goal.

Much of your success will be based on pursuing the right opportunities. Remember not to use the old SWOT analysis, and realize there will always be outside threats and company weaknesses that don't warrant fixing. Rather, focus on opportunities that leverage your strengths, and build your strengths further so they give you sustainable, long-term advantages.

To successfully grow your business, you will need a scorecard. Your scorecard, or financial dashboard, must include the KPIs that underlie your success. For example, tracking both the number of proposals you give and your proposal conversion rates are critical to improving your sales results. Think about the KPIs you would want to know if buying a competing business and ensure you religiously track them in your own.

Although hitting your periodic financial goals is important, building the right business assets is even more so. The right business assets, such as a new product you developed, can reap your company years of financial success. Oftentimes these business assets require an outlay of time or cash and no immediate ROI. Long term, however, they provide the basis of your success, so don't neglect them.

If your business can't operate without you, it's not a business. Instead it's a job, and possibly a miserable one. To solve this, systematize your business. When you do, your business will start to work for you, not the other way around. Your time will be freed to build the business to the next level. This will also cause the value of your systematized business, whether you want to eventually sell it or continue to run it yourself, to skyrocket.

Improving your marketing plan is the easiest and quickest way to boost your sales and profits. Building the right marketing system will allow you to seamlessly attract and turn prospective customers into lifelong customers who dramatically improve the value of your business. Track your results closely and methodically improve each aspect of your marketing system, such as your response rates, conversion rates, transaction prices, and repurchase rates. As you do this, pursue new marketing channels that allow you to gain more customers to whom your competitors simply don't have access.

If you want your business to work for you, you must have the right structure and team in place. Remember to create your three org charts—your endgame, current, and annual org charts, the latter of which is the organization you plan to build within the next year. Continue to build and train your team so that your business runs smoothly and profitably, and you can focus more on growing versus maintaining the business.

Ask your employees how they think their performance should be judged. Make sure that agrees with your thinking. If employees don't understand what success is, they can't possibly achieve it.

Be sure to document your strategic plan. Use it to get everyone in your company focused on one set of goals. Meet monthly to judge your performance against the plan and adjust the goals for the next month and quarter to reflect performance, market shifts, and new ideas as applicable.

Become more rigorous with regard to how you manage your time. Realize how valuable your time is and needs to be to achieve your end vision. Schedule your days to ensure you are constantly completing high value-added tasks that progress your company. Lead and motivate your employees to do the same and to achieve the vision of which they are also a part.

Finally, as simple as it seems, do more of the things that are proven to work and less of the things that haven't worked.

Throughout the book, I referenced the New York Giants as a sports organization that has embodied many of the lessons taught herein. The Giants are constantly thinking about their endgame: How to get to and win the Super Bowl. The team sets tons of financial metric goals (e.g., points scored) and builds business assets, including finding, hiring, and training the right coaches and players. Their management clearly knows how to motivate its players and get them to perform.

Interestingly, although I'm a New Yorker, the Giants are not my favorite football team—the New York Jets are. But whereas the Giants have been able to win two Super Bowls in the last few years alone, the Jets haven't won any in my lifetime. The point is: If you want to win, you not only need to follow the right plan, but you need to execute on it well.

You should now have a business plan to follow that allows you to achieve your goals for the next year and moves you much closer to your ultimate business vision. Make your plan the scoreboard that hangs in your stadium that you watch and review to see how you're doing and that shows you when you need to modify your strategy and priorities to ensure you win the game. Because you can win. And you've already taken the first steps.

ACKNOWLEDGMENTS

Start at the End is the culmination of years of work and experience building my own companies and helping thousands of entrepreneurs and business owners achieve success. I couldn't have done that or written this book without the help of many others.

To start, I'd like to thank my beautiful wife, Kristy, and my kids, Max and Isabella. They are my true *why*. The reason I work so hard to achieve success as an entrepreneur and to help others is so that I can have the freedom to spend as much time as possible with them and travel wherever we want to go. I love each of you more than you'll ever know, and every day, you inspire me to better myself. I'd also like to thank our dog, Hazel, solely because my kids would be upset if I didn't.

Major kudos goes out to Jay Turo, my cofounder at Growthink. I couldn't ask for a better cofounder. In addition to being a brilliant businessman, Jay is one of the most caring and ethical people I've ever met. Jay and I worked on our first business plan together while earning our MBAs at UCLA in 1997, and since then Jay has been responsible for managing Growthink's consulting practice, constantly thinking about and improving how business owners can create and use business plans to achieve more success. Thanks to Jay's wife, Shelmin, and kids, Jay Jay and Teddy, for their hospitality when I make trips to Growthink's Los Angeles office.

Many thanks to my parents, Alan and Brenda, who have always given me unwavering support. Like many entrepreneurs, I started my first venture as a teenager, and my parents were always there to support me. Special thanks to Grandpa Larry, my family's original entrepreneur. Larry started sweeping floors at a ribbon manufacturing plant. Twenty years later he owned the company. The world has been a better place for the last 100 years with Larry in it. Thanks, Larry, for all the inspiring stories from your days in the ribbon business, and thanks to Grandma Ethel for her support and for keeping everyone in line.

I'd also like to thank the entire Growthink team. I don't want to list individual names because there are too many great Growthinkers who do so much. All of them, the entire Growthink team, allowed me to write this book by running the business without me. Thanks to your great work, we've learned new ways to help businesses become more successful. You've touched the lives of thousands of business owners and entrepreneurs throughout the world; lives that will be improved by your advice and caring.

Thanks as well to all the business owners and entrepreneurs who have trusted their businesses to Growthink and followed our advice. This includes our consulting clients, those who have purchased our products, and those who subscribe to our *Growing Your Empire* newsletter, among others. Your support, loyalty, and wisdom is very much appreciated. Kudos to each of you for taking action on the strategies and plans we've discussed and executing on your businesses.

Likewise, I'd like to acknowledge you. Yes, you. You are reading or have read this book to better yourself. To achieve more success. And I commend you on that and wish you the best of luck!

Finally, I'd like to thank the people who most directly allowed this book to come to fruition. Specifically, thanks to Stacey Glick, my literary agent, who is also one of my oldest and best friends in the world. Stacey, you're the best.

Extreme thanks to everyone at John Wiley & Sons, Inc., most notably my editors, Adrianna Johnson and Christine Moore. Both of you helped me so much with your words of encouragement, your massive amounts of comments and good ideas (which I must admit was overwhelming at first), and your commitment to working with me to jointly create a quality product. Thank you so much. You are both great.

ABOUT THE AUTHOR

Dave Lavinsky is a serial entrepreneur and internationally renowned expert in developing business plans that help companies achieve rapid growth.

In 1999, Dave cofounded Growthink, Inc., a consulting and publishing firm. Dave serves as the company's president. Over the past decade, Growthink has written business plans for more than 2,500 clients. Growthink has also helped more than 500,000 other entrepreneurs and business owners to start, grow, or exit their companies via advice on business planning, capital raising, and growth strategies.

In addition to Growthink, Dave has started and exited multiple Internet and product-focused ventures, including Emerge Juice and Nutrition Systems, a wellness products developer and distributor; Shoutmouth, a niche music-focused social networking site; Z Reporter LLC, owner of more than 3,000 niche-focused information websites; and TopPayingKeywords, a search engine marketing and optimization research data firm.

Dave has also published articles and been interviewed in numerous media sources, including *The Wall Street Journal, The New York Times, CNNMoney, Entrepreneur Magazine, Inc. Magazine, The Los Angeles Times,* and *BusinessWeek.*

Dave holds an MBA from the Anderson School of Management at the University of California, Los Angeles, and a bachelor's degree from the University of Virginia. He lives in New York with his wife and two children.

INDEX